Illustrator:
Howard Chaney

Editor:
Marsha Kearns

Editorial Project Manager:
Ina Massler Levin, M.A.

Editor in Chief:
Sharon Coan, M.S. Ed.

Art Director:
Elayne Roberts

Art Coordination Assistant
Cheri Macoubrie Wilson

Cover Artist:
Sue Fullam

Production Manager:
Phil Garcia

Imaging:
Ralph Olmedo, Jr.

Publishers:
Rachelle Cracchiolo, M.S. Ed.
Mary Dupuy Smith, M.S. Ed.

Interdisciplinary Unit
Ancient Rome
CHALLENGING

Author:

Michelle Breyer, M.A.

Teacher Created Materials, Inc.
6421 Industry Way
Westminster, CA   92683
ISBN-1-55734-576-7

©1998 Teacher Created Materials, Inc.   Made in U.S.A.

Table of Contents

Historical Overview—Important Dates: B.C. and A.D.—Main Events in Ancient Roman History—Map of the Roman Empire—Comparison Chart—The Legend of Romulus and Remus—Write About the Legend of Romulus and Remus

The Geography of Ancient Rome—Vocabulary and Comprehension—Make a Physical Feature Map of Ancient Rome—Map of Ancient Rome—The Climate of Ancient Rome

Enid the Etruscan—Vocabulary and Comprehension—Cultural Contributions of Others—Putting People on the Map—Build an Etruscan Arch

Checks and Balances in the Roman Republic—The Republic and Beyond—Vocabulary and Comprehension—The Rights of the People—Comparison Writing: The Republic vs. Democracy—The Writing Process—Editing Checklist—Compare and Contrast Chart—The Punic Wars—Cause and Effect—Publish a Newspaper—Draft a Peace Treaty—You Were There

Julius Caesar—Vocabulary and Comprehension—Make a Personal Timeline—Autobiographical Incident Organizer—Give a Persuasive Speech—Persuasive Speech Organizer—Speech Evaluation Form—Julius Caesar, Mark Antony, and Cleopatra—Mark Antony Speaks—Octavian/Augustus Caesar—Compare Julius and Augustus Caesar—Dramatic Dialogue—What's in a Name?—Emperors of the Pax Romana and Beyond—Create Living Statues—Speech Organizer—Constantine–Comprehension and Debates

Legacies of the Ancient Romans—Our Legacy—Roman Architecture—Make a Simple Sundial—Design a Personal Coin

Latida, a Roman Lady of Leisure—Vocabulary and Comprehension—A Day in the Life—Design a Mail Order Catalog—Compare Weddings—Weddings in Ancient Rome—Make Samian Pottery

The Economy and Trade of Ancient Rome—Chart the Economy and Trade of Ancient Rome—The Roman Empire's Resources—Graph the Empire's Resources—Map the Empire's Resources—A Sea Captain's Log

Table of Contents *(cont.)*

Introduction

Ancient Rome is a uniquely exciting interdisciplinary unit. Its pages are filled with a wide variety of lesson ideas, as well as reproducible pages for use with intermediate and middle school students. The Ancient Rome theme is connected to the curriculum with activities in reading, writing, oral language, science, social studies, math, art, music, and life skills. Many of these activities encourage cooperative learning.

This unit is divided into the following sections to allow for easy thematic planning: Geography, Early Roman Cultures, Government (The Roman Republic, The Punic Wars, Great Leaders of the Roman Empire), Science and Achievements, Social Structure and Family Life, Economy and Trade, Religion, Education, The Arts and Entertainment, The Fall of the Roman Empire, and Literature Connection. The lessons are designed so that they can be used in conjunction with social studies textbooks.

This interdisciplinary unit includes the following:

- **Curriculum Connections**—lessons that incorporate math, science, language arts, fine arts, and social studies

- **Visual and Performing Arts**—activities for creating Roman mosaics, murals, speeches, drama, and music

- **Group Projects and Activities**—to help foster cooperative learning strategies and critical thinking skills

- **Bulletin Board Ideas**—motivational, interactive, and informative board ideas as well as duplicate pages to create overhead transparencies for informational charts, pictures, etc.

- **Moments in Time**—reading selections, readers theaters, and reenactments to transport the student back to the days of Ancient Rome

- **Literature Connection:** *How Would You Survive as an Ancient Roman?*—a nonfiction book and related activities that lead your class through a simulation of life in Ancient Rome. This book is filled with interesting facts and trivia not always included in history books. The lessons immerse students in the study of Ancient Rome by giving them a role to play in Ancient Roman society and activities that correspond to that role. The sequence of the literature lessons follows the format of this unit, so it is easy to incorporate the literature connection lessons after you teach each section of the unit. Or you may wish to utilize the Literature Connection lessons at one time as the foundation of an extensive culminating activity.

Moments in Time—Readers' Theater

Along with nonfiction passages of text, information for most sections of study is provided in the form of a short "play" to be read aloud by the class. This allows the students to experience a "moment in time" by being transported back to the days of the Ancient Romans and makes learning more creative and fun. Assign parts to different students and have them read the selections aloud to the class. Have the class study the pictures and discuss what life was like for the Ancient Romans. Vocabulary and comprehension questions or activities accompany each readers' theater.

Historical Overview

To begin the unit on Ancient Rome, give students a broad understanding of the political changes that occurred during the two thousand years the Roman Empire dominated the Mediterranean region.

Preparing for the lesson:

1. Reproduce Ancient Rome—Important Dates (pages 8–9) for each student.

2. Reproduce Main Events in Ancient Roman History and Map of the Roman Empire (pages 10–11) for each student.

3. You may wish to make the copies for (1.) and (2.) above two-sided so students can more easily retain and use them as you study the unit.

Teaching the lesson:

1. Discuss with the class what they already know about Ancient Rome.

2. Give students a copy of Important Dates—B.C. and A.D. and have them refer to it as you read aloud the Historical Overview information on pages 6–7.

3. Lead the class in a general discussion of the Roman/Christian calendar as it applies to how we now denote the time before the birth of Jesus Christ as B.C. (years counted backwards) and the time during and after his life as A.D. (years counted forward).

4. Explain to students that Ancient Rome experienced many changes during its approximately 2,000-year history. Discuss what they now know about changes in government and religion, and brainstorm with the class about the kinds of cultural changes that might have occurred as Rome expanded into foreign territories.

5. Distribute the Main Events in Ancient Roman History and Map of the Roman Empire to students. Tell them that they will be learning more about these main events during your study of this unit. Have them use their copies of Important Dates to write the specific dates on the Main Events timeline.

6. Discuss with the class the Map of the Roman Empire. Tell them that as you study about Ancient Rome, they will add important information to the map to create a more detailed and comprehensive picture of the rise and fall of the Roman Empire.

7. Throughout the unit refer students to the important dates, main events, and map.

Historical Overview *(cont.)*

The early Romans believed a legend that claims a youth named Romulus founded the city of Rome. Historical evidence tells us that the original inhabitants of the region were simple peasant farmers called Latins who migrated to the area from Central Europe and settled along the banks of the Tiber River. In this central part of Italy the city of Rome grew to become the center of a vast empire. At its peak, the Roman Empire stretched from the Atlantic Ocean in the west to the Caspian Sea in the east. It reached northward into Britain and southward into Egypt.

While the Latins occupied the area around Rome, three other powers moved in around them. The Etruscans moved into central and northern Italy. The Greeks crossed into southern Italy. The powerful Carthaginians expanded into northern Africa. These different cultures would make lasting contributions to Roman culture and history.

Rome was ruled by kings during its first two centuries. When the Romans finally were able to defeat the last Etruscan king in 509 B.C., they formed a new kind of government called a republic. In this system the elected leaders were advised by a group of men from the more powerful families.

The citizens of the Roman Republic were divided into two classes. The upper-class of noblemen and their families were called patricians. These men could hold political, military, or religious offices. The plebeians were the common people who comprised most of the population. For years the plebeians struggled with the patricians for equality and power.

As the Roman army marched off to expand the Republic's holdings, it waged war with many neighbors. Carthage had established many successful trading posts around the Mediterranean. Rome and Carthage became bitter rivals and fought three long and bloody battles, called the Punic Wars, in order to dominate the Mediterranean region. Rome finally defeated Carthage in 146 B.C. and became the sole ruler of a mighty and gigantic empire.

How was Rome able to conquer and control so much territory and unite it under one rule? There are five main reasons.

1. Romans loved their Republic and defended it with fierce patriotic determination. They took great pride in their military successes, and they continued building and strengthening their army with the spoils of their victories.

2. Once a region became a Roman province, many of the native people were granted Roman citizenship. They then gained the benefits of Roman protection and stability. In turn, Rome taxed the people to help pay for a stronger army.

3. The Romans absorbed the achievements of the people they conquered and utilized them to help develop a lifestyle that was often more advanced and comfortable than before. Many people liked the advantages of this and willingly adopted Roman rule.

4. The Romans allowed people in conquered regions to keep their own language and religion, as long as they also worshipped Roman gods and learned Latin, the official Roman language.

5. The Romans were excellent engineers and builders. They constructed a vast network of roads throughout the Empire that allowed for more efficient travel and trade.

Historical Overview *(cont.)*

As Rome aggressively expanded its Empire, civil wars were common. Warlords fought amongst themselves, and slaves rebelled against the Roman Army. Dishonest and greedy leaders fought one another for control of the government. One such leader was Julius Caesar. He had been a successful general in the army. Back home, Caesar fought for and gained great power. He declared himself dictator. Fearing Caesar's disregard for Rome's constitution, a group of senators assassinated him. However, their hopes of saving the Republic did not materialize. Caesar's death only caused a greater struggle for power.

For several years Caesar's adopted son, Octavian, shared power with Mark Antony and Queen Cleopatra of Egypt. After defeating the Egyptians, Octavian ruled as the first emperor of Rome under the name of Augustus Caesar. Although his rule marked the end of the Republic, it also began a new era of Pax Romana, or Roman peace, and the beginning of centuries of rule by emperors.

The birth of Jesus Christ marked the change between the time eras we know as B.C. and A.D. The rapid growth, spread, and influence of religion in the area—mainly Christianity and Judaism—created much fear within the Roman government. Many Christians were persecuted and even put to death. Pontius Pilate ordered the crucifixion of Jesus Christ in about A.D. 30. The first Christian emperor did not come to power until A.D. 306. He was Constantine the Great, who ruled until A.D. 337.

After Constantine's rule ended, pagan religions were forbidden and their followers were persecuted. The mighty Roman Empire was permanently divided into East (Byzantine) and West. The Empire's weakening power allowed for more conquest by invading barbarians. Around A.D. 475, the Western Empire collapsed. What followed in this area was an era of unrest and turmoil known as the Dark Ages. However, the Eastern Empire continued to flourish and lasted another thousand years before it fell to the Turks. The once-great Roman Empire finally ended in A.D. 1453.

Important Dates—B.C.

Ruled by Kings

700s	Historical founding of Rome, exact date unknown
753	Legendary founding of Rome by Romulus
509	Rome rebels against the Etruscan kings and establishes a Republic

Ruled by Republic

494	Plebeians revolt against the patrician class in Rome
450	The Twelve Tablets (Roman Laws) are displayed in the Forum
390	Invasion of the Gauls (French)
340–285	Wars with the Etruscans, Samnites, and Gauls
287	Plebeians withdraw from Rome to gain equity under Roman law
264–241	First Punic War aginst Carthage
241–225	Rome seizes the islands of Sicily, Sardinia, and Corsica
218–202	Second Punic War—Hannibal uses elephants to cross the Alps and invade Rome
200–125	Roman provinces established in Spain, Southern France, Greece, Macedonia, Turkey, and Northern Africa
149–146	Third Punic War—Roman Army destroys Carthage
100–31	Civil wars between warlords
73–71	Sparticus leads slave uprising against the Roman Army
58–51	Julius Caesar conquers Gaul
50	Rome controls entire Mediterranean region
49–46	Julius Caesar and troops cross the Rubicon River, causing and winning a civil war; Caesar declares himself dictator of Rome for life
44	Caesar assassinated; in Rome, Octavian shares the control of the Roman Empire with Mark Antony and Queen Cleopatra, in Egypt
42–30	Civil wars begin anew
31	Octavian defeats Mark Antony
30	Mark Antony and Cleopatra commit suicide to prevent being taken back to Rome
27	Reign of Octavian, first emperor and now called Augustus Caesar; end of the Republic

Birth of Jesus Christ

Important Dates—A.D.

Birth of Jesus Christ

26–36	Pontius Pilate orders the crucifixion of Jesus Christ (around A.D. 30)
37–41	Reign of Caligula
41–54	Reign of Claudius, conquest of Britain
54–68	Reign of Nero, great fire in Rome blamed on the Christians
68–69	Civil wars
79	Eruption of Mt. Vesuvius destroys the city of Pompeii
100's	Pax Romana, peaceful and prosperous period
230–284	Trade declines; chaos in the Empire; wars with Persians and Germans; civil wars
250	Worship of the emperor and Roman gods made compulsory, Christians who refused were killed
268	Goth invasion; Corinth and Sparta sacked
284–305	Reign of Diocletian; division of Empire into Western (Rome) and Eastern (Byzantine); peaceful time
306–337	Reign of Constantine the Great, who reunites the Empire; first Christian emperor, makes Christianity tolerated throughout the Empire; establishes Constantinople as the capital of the Empire
391	Pagan religions forbidden and followers persecuted
395	Empire permanently divided into East and West
400–700	Roman Empire invaded and weakened by invasion of barbarians in 406; Invasion of the Rhine frontier; Germans overrun Gaul (France)
410	Invasion and capture of Rome by Visigoth barbarians
433–453	Invasion by Attila and the Huns
475–476	Romulus Augustulus deposed, Western Roman Empire ends; Dark Age begins; Eastern Empire unaffected
533–554	Eastern Emperor Justinian reconquers Italy and North Africa
634–642	Eastern (Byzantine) Empire loses Egypt and Syria to Islamic armies
1453	Fall of Constantinople to the Ottoman Turks ends the Holy Roman (Byzantine) Empire

Ruled by Emperors

Empire Divided—Eastern/Western

Eastern Empire

Main Events in Ancient Roman History

On the blanks, write the correct dates for each event.

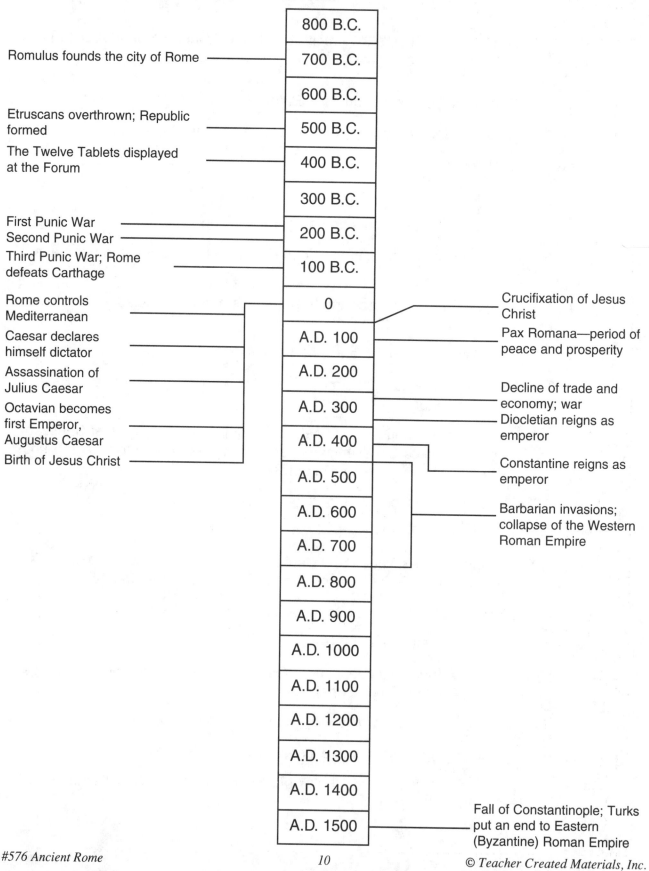

Romulus founds the city of Rome	800 B.C.
	700 B.C.
	600 B.C.
Etruscans overthrown; Republic formed	500 B.C.
The Twelve Tablets displayed at the Forum	400 B.C.
	300 B.C.
First Punic War / Second Punic War	200 B.C.
Third Punic War; Rome defeats Carthage	100 B.C.
Rome controls Mediterranean	0 — Crucifixation of Jesus Christ
Caesar declares himself dictator	A.D. 100 — Pax Romana—period of peace and prosperity
Assassination of Julius Caesar	A.D. 200
Octavian becomes first Emperor, Augustus Caesar	A.D. 300 — Decline of trade and economy; war / Diocletian reigns as emperor
Birth of Jesus Christ	A.D. 400 — Constantine reigns as emperor
	A.D. 500
	A.D. 600 — Barbarian invasions; collapse of the Western Roman Empire
	A.D. 700
	A.D. 800
	A.D. 900
	A.D. 1000
	A.D. 1100
	A.D. 1200
	A.D. 1300
	A.D. 1400
	A.D. 1500 — Fall of Constantinople; Turks put an end to Eastern (Byzantine) Roman Empire

Map of the Roman Empire

Keep this map to refer to as you study about Ancient Rome. Add other important information to the map as you learn it.

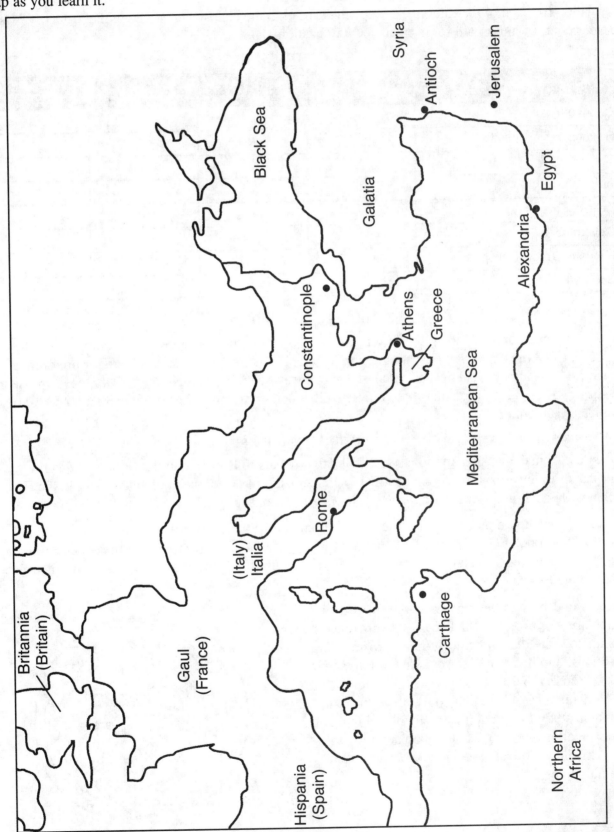

Comparison Chart

If you haven't done so for previous units, make a chart out of two pieces of tagboard to use throughout this unit and future units on ancient civilizations. Use a black marker and index cards to record information for each of the categories. Tape the card onto the chart when studying that category. Use a different color of index card for each ancient civilization.

Comparison Chart

	Middle East	Egypt	Greece	Rome
Geography				
Science/Achievements				
The Arts				
Education				
Religion				
Government				
Economy/Trade/Transportation				
Society/Family				

Motivational Videos

Enhance students' understanding of Ancient Rome by showing one or more videos during the unit. *Sparticus*, *Cleopatra*, and *Ben Hur* are three favorite epics that give a detailed picture of life during Roman rule. You may wish to show each movie over several days, as they may be too long to view in one sitting. Remind students that these reflect Hollywood's version of history and are not necessarily completely authentic.

Vocabulary Books

Have students make vocabulary books in a shape that relates to Roman culture. Find and display examples of such Roman icons as a chariot, a helmet, a suit of armor, head of Julius Caesar, the Forum, a temple, a gladiator, a Roman arch, a vase, the Cross of Constantine, etc.

Give each student two pieces of construction paper and allow them to draw and cut out a front and back cover for their book. Give them 10–15 pieces of writing paper and have them cut the paper out in the same shape as the cover. Have students punch holes and use brads to bind the books. Have them label and decorate their covers.

As you work through the unit, write the suggested vocabulary words on the chalkboard. Allow time for students to write the words, look up and write definitions, and illustrate the words in their vocabulary books. You may wish to assign this as homework. Tell students they will be able to use these books to help them study for the unit assessment and that you may even allow them to use their books during the test. This may motivate them to take accurate and thorough notes.

12

The Legend of Romulus and Remus

Long ago in northern Italy there lived a great king named Numitor, who ruled the city of Alba Longa. The king had a very jealous younger brother, Amulius, who eventually gained a following and seized the throne, sending Numitor into exile. Amulius proved to be a fierce ruler. He spared the life of Rhea Silvea, Numitor's beautiful daughter, but forced her to serve in the palace temple.

One night while she was alone in the temple, Rhea was visited by Mars, the god of war. He immediately fell in love with her, and nine months later she gave birth to twin boys, whom she named Remus and Romulus. She tried to raise the babies in secrecy, but Amulius discovered her deception and became enraged. He ordered all three of them to be thrown into the Tiber River and drowned.

Before she died, Rhea managed to put her babies into a basket. The boys floated safely away downstream. The basket came ashore at Palatine, where a she-wolf happened to be passing by. Upon hearing the soft cries of the babies, she took them back to her den and raised them on her milk. A woodpecker also befriended the boys and brought them fruit, nuts, and meat. From that day forward, the woodpecker and the wolf became the sacred animals of Mars.

The boys grew up strong and healthy. One day a shepherd tending his flock discovered the twins and took them home with him. The good shepherd and his wife raised the twins as their own for ten happy years. The boys were well cared for, and they learned how to read and write. They also helped defend their family against attacks by bandits.

However, there came a time when the family was outnumbered and surrounded by bandits. Romulus managed to escape, but Remus was captured and brought before the bandits' leader. The leader decided to take Remus to the local landowner and turn Remus in as the one who had been attacking and stealing from the community. The landowner was old and the bandits believed he could be easily fooled.

The Legend of Romulus and Remus *(cont.)*

Before passing judgment on the boy, the landowner allowed Remus to tell his story. As Remus spoke, the landowner began to cry. Remus was the grandson he had never known. The landowner was none other than Numitor, the exiled king of Alba Longa. He brought the boys back into their real family, and together they took the throne back from King Amulius. All was well for a time.

After a while, the boys tired of their life in Alba Longa. They wanted to rule a great city of their own. They traveled near and far until they found themselves back in Palatine, where they had washed ashore as babies. They decided it was here they would build a grand city. Romulus felt he was better suited to rule and wanted to name the city Rome. But Remus thought that he would make a better ruler and that Reme was a far better name for a town.

They argued for days until coming up with a solution. Were they not children of a god? Why not let the gods decide who would be king? They climbed to the top of a hill and waited for an omen, or sign, from the gods. Within moments six large vultures soared down from the sky and encircled Remus. Remus shouted triumphantly that he would be king!

His cry had scarcely faded away when to his great surprise twelve giant vultures came down and encircled Romulus. Romulus began to make plans to build the great city of Rome, which he would rule. Unfortunately, Remus was a very poor loser and continually taunted Romulus. Finally, Romulus lost his patience and his temper. He drew his sword and hurled it at his brother. He didn't mean to kill Remus, but the sword pierced Remus's body, and his brother slowly fell to the ground at Romulus's feet. Thus was Rome founded—in a pool of blood.

Although this story is a legend, it helped shape the history of Rome and came to symbolize the rise and fall of the great Roman Empire.

14

Write About the Legend of Romulus and Remus

Imagine that you are one of the characters from the legend of Romulus and Remus. Pretend that you have kept a diary all your life. Choose an important event from your life and write about it from your perspective. Be sure to describe what happened, your feelings, and how you reacted to the event. You may wish to consider the suggestions below. When you have finished your diary entry, trade with a partner and read his or her entry. Discuss how you felt upon reading the other's diary.

King Numitor: losing the throne to your brother; starting a new life alone; finding your grandsons; working with your grandsons to regain your throne; saying good-bye to your grandsons again as they leave to search for their own place; hearing about the death of Remus

Rhea Silvea: having your father exiled from the city; being forced to work in the temple; meeting Mars, the god of war; having your babies in secret; being discovered by Amulius; saving your babies' lives by putting them in a basket in the Tiber River

King Amulius: your feelings toward your older brother; plotting to take away the throne; sending away your brother and putting your niece to work in the temple; discovering the twins; sending your brother's family to drown in the river; ruling your kingdom; being overthrown by Numitor, Remus, and Romulus several years later

The shepherd or his wife: finding the twins; learning they had been raised by a wolf and woodpecker; taking them home; being attacked by bandits; losing Remus to bandits; losing both boys to their natural grandfather, Numitor; hearing of Romulus's fortune and Remus's death

Remus or Romulus: life with the wolf and woodpecker; life with the shepherd and his wife; fighting bandits; finding your grandfather, Numitor; winning back the throne; leaving in search of your own place; waiting for an omen from the gods; Romulus becoming king; the accidental killing of Remus

The Geography of Ancient Rome

Italy is a rocky, mountainous peninsula 600 miles long and 150 miles wide. The **Apennine Mountains** form its "backbone" and stretch from north to south, with the **Tiber River** cutting through them in central Italy. Along the northern border, the **Alps** serve as a natural boundary. The three major bodies of water surrounding Italy are the **Adriatic Sea**, the **Ionian Sea**, and the **Mediterranean Sea**. Romans developed many trade routes to other regions in the Mediterranean region. Greece is only 50 miles away, across the Adriatic Sea, and Africa is only 100 miles from the west coast of **Sicily**.

Along the western coast of Italy, at the base of the Apennine mountain range, lie three plains areas. Here are where most early people settled. The **Tuscan Plains** in the north, drained by the **Po River**, were a fertile farming region. The **Latium Plains** became the home of **Alba Longa** and **Rome**, bustling cities near the Tiber River and the seacoast, hub of the Roman Empire's trade business. The southern plains area, the **Campanian**, boasted Italy's best harbor.

The Italian peninsula was perfect for a consolidation of power within Italy and an expansion of power from Italy to other parts of the area. It was in the Latium Plains that an Indo-European tribe called Latins first settled. These people were the early ancestors of the Romans. Their first city, Alba Longa, was established around 1000 B.C. Their most important city, Rome, was founded in 753 B.C. by Romulus.

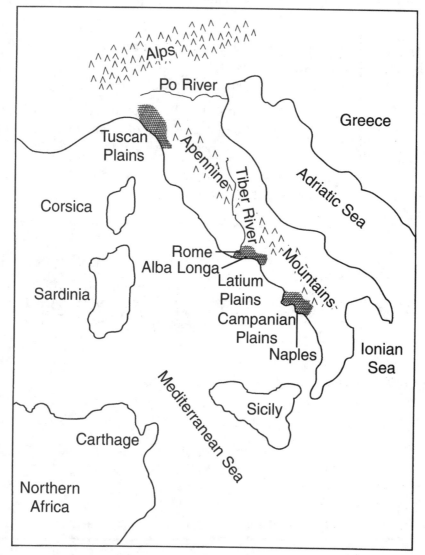

The Geography of Ancient Rome *(cont.)*

What did the early settlers look for when deciding where to build their cities, and how did the site chosen for Rome fit these criteria?

Fresh Water—Fresh water is essential for all life—people, animals, and crops. Rivers also provide a means for trade and transportation.

Sea Access—Ports are necessary to safely harbor the ships used for trade and military expansion into other lands.

Good Land—For a city to flourish, it must be out of flood range and have land good for farming, grazing, and hunting.

Protection—The site chosen for a major city must offer protection from invaders by land or by sea. It must also provide room for growth and expansion.

Rome was built 15 miles inland on the crest of seven hills covered with forests of oak and chestnut. Small streams ran through the valleys, and flanking the seven hills was the large Tiber River, whose steep banks served as additional natural protection. The Mediterranean climate of hot, dry summers and wet, mild winters proved ideal for people, plants, and animals. The rich volcanic soil was perfect for raising crops.

From Rome's vantage point the Roman Empire began and grew. Many large cities were established, but most of the people lived in **farming communities** and worked the land. These communities consisted of small villages, farmsteads, and hamlets. Farm workers produced the food, materials, and fuel that the large cities needed. It was a difficult life of endless work for men, women, and children.

The very rich in Ancient Rome owned vast estates of fertile farmland. Here they built magnificent **villas** to which they would flee to escape the heat and congestion of the cities where they conducted their business. The estates were cared for by slaves, whose lives were grindingly hard and far removed from the peaceful and luxurious country life their owners enjoyed.

On farmland near the warm shores of the **Mediterranean Sea** farmers grew many grains, such as emmer wheat, which was made into bread and used in other foods. It was highly nutritious, with almost twice as much protein as modern wheat today. But as the Roman Empire grew, it could not feed all of its people alone, so wheat and other grains were imported from Egypt and other areas in northern Africa.

The Geography of Ancient Rome *(cont.)*

The most prized crops were grapes and olives, both of which grew well in the rocky soil and warm climate. Grapes were fermented and made into wine. There were few other beverages available, so wine was widely consumed throughout the Mediterranean region and was therefore a valuable trade commodity. Olives were grown to be eaten and also to be processed for their oil. Olive oil became a basic essential for Mediterranean cooking. It was also used as fuel in lamps and for cleaning the body.

Large ranches with pigs, cattle, goats, and sheep were able to thrive in regions unsuitable for planting. Large cattle ranches provided meat, leather goods, and dairy products. Goats and sheep produced milk, cheese, meat, and the wool used for clothing. Hunting wild animals such as boar and deer was a favorite, though dangerous, sport for many Romans. In addition to offering good hunting, the forests were valuable for their wood for building and for fuel. Fish and waterfowl were plentiful. In short, because of Italy's natural resources—and its hard-working people—the Ancient Romans were able to establish and maintain a far-reaching civilization that lasted nearly 2,000 years.

18

Vocabulary and Comprehension

Write the following words on the chalkboard for students to copy into their vocabulary books. Remind students to define and illustrate each word.

Apennine Mountains	**Ionian Sea**	**Rome**
Alba Longa	**Latium Plains**	**Tiber River**
Alps	**Mediterranean Sea**	**Tuscan Plains**
Adriatic Sea	**Po River**	**farming communities**
Campanian	**Sicily**	**villas**

Use all or some of the following questions for whole-class discussion, small-group work, or individual assessment. Allow students to refer back to the story while working.

1. What are the mountain ranges of Italy, and what benefits did they provide the Ancient Romans? *(The Alps and the Apennine Mountains provided protection and natural resources.)*

2. What main advantage did the Italian peninsula offer for establishing an empire? *(The seas opened trade to many new areas and provided a way for the military to go to and conquer other lands.)*

3. Why were new settlements built along rivers? *(Rivers provided fresh water for people, plants, and animals; they also provided a means of trade and transportation.)*

4. Why was the location of Rome so ideal? *(Rome's location on the Tiber River provided a means for trade and transportation and was a source of fresh water; the volcanic soil was fertile; it was far enough inland to provide protection from enemy invasion; access to the sea made it good for a trade and military center.)*

5. What different types of farms flourished on the Italian peninsula? *(Farms for growing wheat, olives, and grapes; ranches for raising cattle, pigs, goats, and sheep.)*

6. How was life different for those who owned large farming estates and those who actually worked the land? *(Working the land was hard labor and was performed by slaves; the estate owners worked in the cities and came to the country to relax, not to work.)*

Make a Physical Feature Map of Ancient Rome

Use the map on page 21 and the directions below to make a map showing the physical features of Ancient Rome.

1. Locate, draw, and label the Apennine Mountains and the Alps. Color these two mountain ranges brown.

2. Label the Mediterranean Sea, the Adriatic Sea, and the Ionian Sea. Color the seas blue.

3. Locate, draw, and label the Tiber River and the Po River. Color the rivers blue.

4. Locate and label the islands of Corsica, Sardinia, and Sicily. Color the islands yellow.

5. Locate, draw, and label the Tuscan Plain, the Latium Plain, and Campanian Plain. Color the plains green.

6. Color the rest of the Italian coastline yellow.

7. Locate and label Northern Africa.

8. Locate, indicate, and label the cities of Rome, Alba Longa, and Naples.

9. Make a compass rose on your map showing north, south, east, and west.

10. Make a map key showing what each symbol and color represents on your map.

11. Make a scale showing that 1 inch equals 100 miles.

12. Cut out your map and glue it onto a sheet of colored construction paper.

13. At the top clearly write The Geography of Ancient Rome and your name.

Map of Ancient Rome

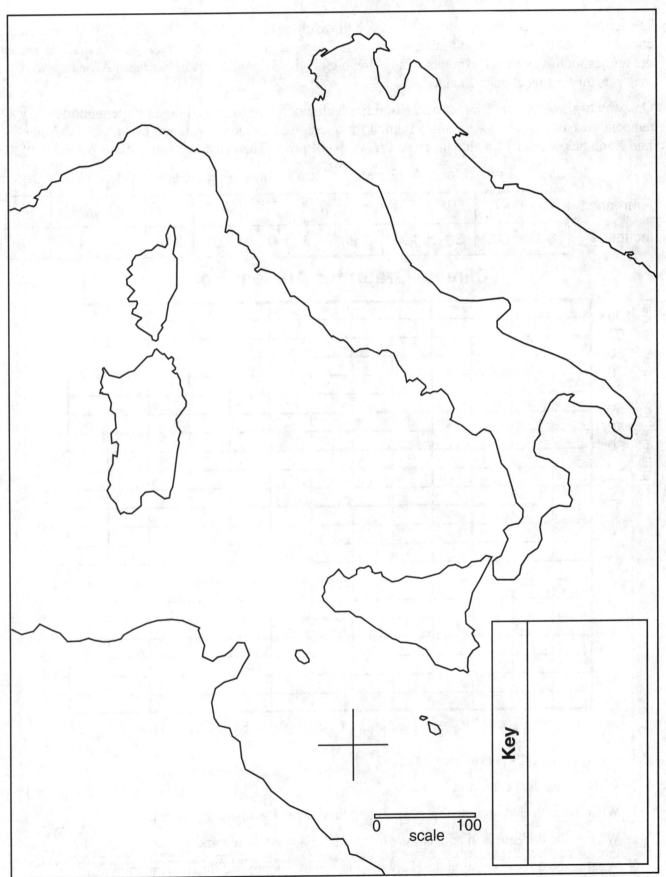

Key

0   scale   100

The Climate of Ancient Rome

The term "climate" describes a general year-round weather pattern. Most of Italy has a Mediterranean climate of hot, dry summers and mild, wet winters. Temperatures tend to increase and rainfall decrease the farther south you travel. The hot winds blowing off the Sahara Desert in Northern Africa are a major factor for this climate change.

One way to show climate is in a graph. To make a climate graph you need the average monthly temperatures and the average monthly rainfall for a region. Use the information in the table and the line graph below to make a climate graph for Ancient Rome. Then answer the questions below.

	Jan.	Feb.	Mar.	April	May	June	July	Aug.	Sept.	Oct.	Nov.	Dec.
Fahrenheit	45°	47°	50°	57°	64°	71°	77°	77°	70°	62°	54°	47°
Inches	3.1	3.5	3.1	2.4	2.2	1.5	0.2	0.9	2.6	4.8	4.8	3.6

Climate Graph for Ancient Rome

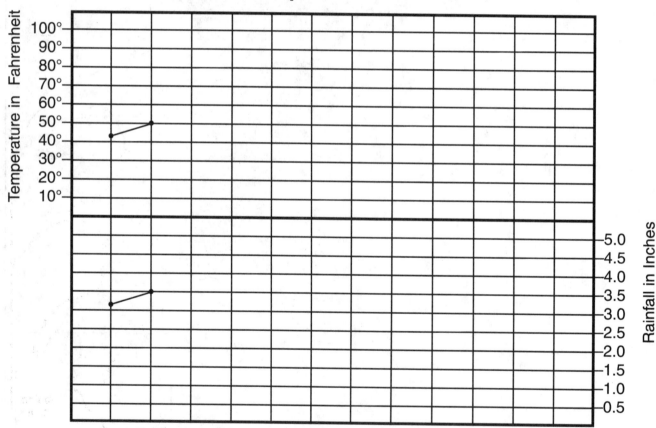

1. What two months get the most rainfall?

2. What season is the warmest?

3. What overall trend do you notice with the rainfall as the temperature increases?

4. What is the difference in temperature between the hottest month and the coolest month?

5. What is the difference in rainfall between the wettest month and the driest month?

Enid the Etruscan

Narrators 1–6	**Pietre**—patrician
Narrator	**Enid, Lathe,** and **Tareme**—Etruscans
Harid—Carthaginian	**Claudius**—Latin/Roman
Theopompus, Tyre, and	
Hector—Greeks	

Narrator: The original ancestors of the Romans were the **Latins**. They were an Indo-European tribe who settled in central Italy south of the Tiber River. The Latins were strongly influenced by the **Greeks** and **Etruscans** who also inhabited the peninsula. The **Carthaginians** from northern Africa helped to shape the culture of the future Romans as well. Travel to a cafe in modern-day Italy. Here, in a bustling place filled with many different types of people, descendants of these early people discuss their ancestors' roles in creating the Roman Empire.

Enid: It's true that Rome profited greatly from all its neighbors. I'm glad that even back then her citizens had the insight to learn from the knowledge, customs, and beliefs of the various cultures they encountered. Of course, it was my ancestors, the Etruscans, who contributed the most.

Tareme: Yes, our ancestors arrived on the Italian coast north of the Tiber River around 800 B.C. Most scholars believe they migrated from Asia Minor. They settled inland in an area known as Etruria, which today is known as the provinces of Tuscany and Umbria. Our people were hard and warlike and became a powerful force. They traded along the western coast and established cities all over northern and central Italy, from the Po River Valley to the Latium Plains. Eventually they developed codes of law, built a profitable trade, and encouraged art. The Etruscans also established colonies on Corsica and Sardinia, where they set up trade with the Carthaginians. They are considered the first real civilized people in Italy.

Lathe: In 575 B.C. the Etruscans expanded into the area of Rome, overpowered the Romans, and ruled for the next 66 years. By this time their navy dominated the seas and their culture was the most brilliant ever seen in Italy.

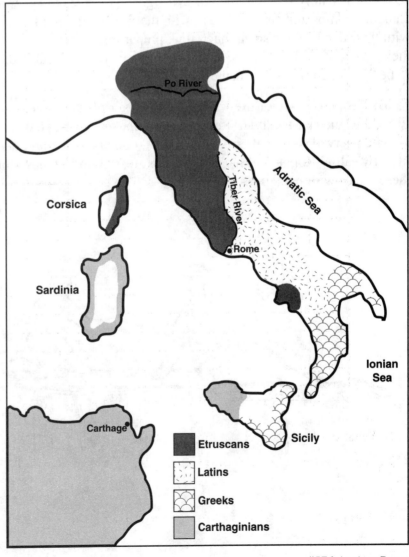

Enid the Etruscan *(cont.)*

Enid: It was the Etruscans who actually taught the Romans how to build and spread the Empire, through architecture and engineering. They were the first to build the famous arches made of wedge-shaped stones held together only by the pressure of one stone against the other. They then passed this knowledge on to the Romans, who used them in their temples, bridges, and government buildings. The Etruscans also passed along their engineering skills by teaching the Romans how to build roads, bridges, homes, and aqueducts. The Romans took these skills and used them far more extensively than ever before.

Tareme: It was also the Etruscans who helped the Romans develop a strong military. Etruria was rich in iron ore and the people were skilled at working with metals. Their weapons were far superior to those of their opponents. The Etruscans had armies of well-trained and disciplined soldiers. The Romans adopted Etruscan fighting techniques, weapons, and armor, becoming so proficient in their use that they were able to overpower the Etruscans in the 4th century B.C.

Lathe: And don't forget religion. The Etruscans were almost fanatically religious people who spent a great deal of time making offerings to their primitive gods, examining entrails, or studying weather patterns for omens. It was through this influence that the Romans became a highly superstitious people, constantly seeking good or evil signs in everyday happenings. The Etruscans also built elaborate tombs and supplied them with the necessities and luxuries of life, much like the Egyptians did with their dead. They spent much time preparing for death so that their spirits could live on and enjoy their lavish lifestyle. Their sarcophagi were elaborately sculpted, and their funerary art styles continued to be developed by the Romans.

Enid: Yes, their love of life was evident in their pleasure-seeking ways. The Romans adopted the Etruscans' elegant lifestyle. Reclining on couches at banquets to watch dancers and other entertainers as slaves served course after course of fine food and drink at lavish dinner parties became a part of the life of wealthy Romans. Men and women dressed up in fancy clothes, jewelry, and make-up to enjoy these meals with neighbors.

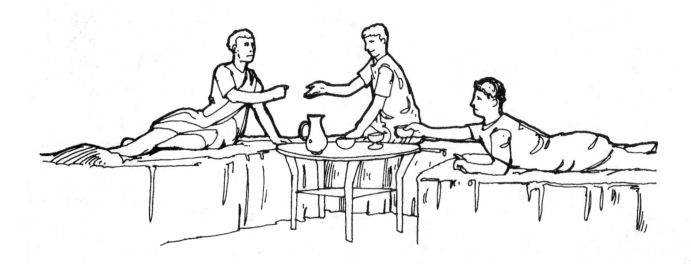

24

Enid the Etruscan *(cont.)*

Theopompus: The Etruscans also developed women's rights. They gave women much more freedom than my ancestors, the Greeks, did. Etruscan women were considered equal to their men. They could go out alone. They ate with the men and learned how to read. Sometimes they owned property, and they had great influence over the men and their decision making. Roman women also enjoyed many of the same privileges. Although the Romans did not adopt many of the restrictive social customs of the Greeks, they did base much of their culture on Greek ways.

Hector: As early as 600 B.C. the Greeks had established colonies in southern Italy and on the island of Sicily. Since they were there to civilize the people and not to conquer them, they introduced the Latin tribes to the skills and fine craftsmanship of the East. The Greek influence grew even stronger when Rome conquered Greece.

Tyre: The Greeks were considered outstanding in the arts, literature, and education. Greek statues and paintings were copied. Roman writers often turned to the Greeks for inspiration, admiring the works of their poets, playwrights, and authors of epic tales. Greek scholars were brought to Rome to educate wealthy Roman youths. There has always been a question about the Roman alphabet. Many say it was brought by the Etruscans, but others say the Etruscans adapted it from the Greek alphabet. I guess it could be considered a little of both.

Theopompus: The Romans also borrowed heavily from Greek religion and architecture. They worshipped Greek gods, yet gave them Roman names. They adopted basic Greek forms in architecture, including the use of columns and the triangular pediment.

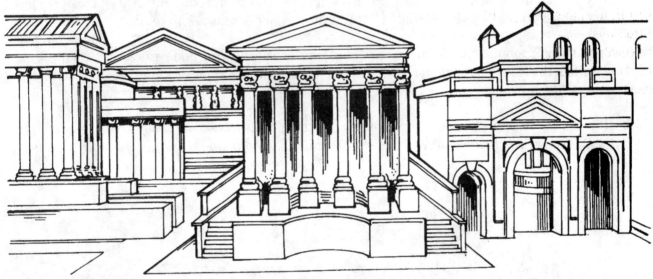

Harid: Let's not forget that there were others—people from North Africa and the islands of Sicily and Sardinia. They were my ancestors, the Carthaginians. They were commercial rivals of Rome and they exercised control over a number of important city-states from their African capital city of Carthage. It was with them that the Romans fought the Punic Wars to establish control of the western Mediterranean area.

Claudius: And it was the Latins, the Romans' original ancestors, who developed a unified language for the Empire. Latin is still used today in such areas as medicine and law. So although the Latins were influenced by the Etruscans and Greeks in developing Roman culture, they also contributed mightily in making the Roman Empire so powerful a force for so long a time.

Vocabulary and Comprehension

Write the following words on the chalkboard for students to copy into their vocabulary books. Remind students to define and illustrate each word.

Latins	**Greeks**	**Carthaginians**	**Etruscans**

Use all or some of the following questions for whole-class discussion, small-group work, or individual assessment. Allow students to refer back to the story while working.

1. Who were the original ancestors of the Romans? (*Latins*)

2. What other people settled in and around Italy? (*Etruscans, Greeks, and Carthaginians*)

3. Why do you think a Greek might have been shocked to meet an Etruscan woman? (*Unlike Greek women, Etruscan women had the freedom to be out in public alone and do things with the men. They could own property and influence the decisions of men.*)

4. The Romans developed a complex systems of roads. From whom did they learn this skill? (*Etruscans*)

5. Why do you think the Romans adopted Greek religion and architecture rather than creating their own unique gods and style of building? (*Accept reasonable answers.*)

6. Do you think adopting the Etruscan social customs of lavish living and parties was wise? Or do you think the Romans should have adopted the Greek ways of simple living? Why? (*Accept reasonable answers.*)

7. How did the Romans benefit from having the Carthaginians as rivals? (*They developed better trade, and the competition developed better military and political skills. Accept other reasonable answers.*)

Cultural Contributions of Others

The Romans profited greatly from their association with their neighbors the Greeks and the Etruscans. Write the list of words on the chalkboard, and guide students to create a contribution chart or web that shows how these two other important cultures influenced the Ancient Romans.

- the alphabet
- funerary art and tombs
- architecture with columns
- engineering skills
- lavish dinner parties

- literature
- religious superstitions
- religion—gods and worship
- strong military

- stone arches
- art and sculpture
- educating youth
- freedoms for women

You may wish to use the following examples of charts or the web.

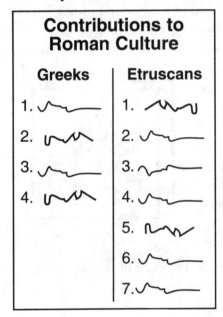

Contributions to Roman Culture

Greeks	Etruscans
1.	1.
2.	2.
3.	3.
4.	4.
	5.
	6.
	7.

Charts ←→

Web ↓

Cultural Contributions

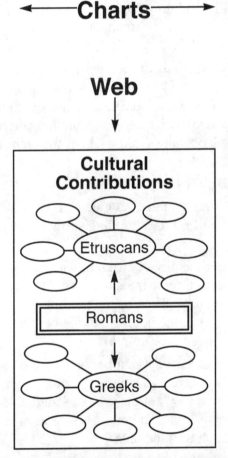

Who Contributed What?

	Greeks	Etruscans
	✓	
		✓
	✓	✓
		✓
		✓
		✓
	✓	✓
	✓	✓

Putting People on the Map

Have students add people to the physical features map they made (page 21). Have them locate and label the areas where the Latins, Etruscans, Carthaginians, and Greeks settled. Remind them to color the separate areas and add to their map key.

Build an Etruscan Arch

One of the many Etruscan contributions to Roman culture was the stone arch. Have students make an Etruscan/Roman arch.

Preparing for the lesson:

1. Divide the class into groups of four students.
2. Reproduce an arch pattern (page 29) for each group.
3. Gather for each group two pieces of cardboard big enough to fit the arch pattern, a heavy-duty pair of scissors, a protractor, glue, a pencil, and a marker.

Teaching the lesson:

1. Tell students to make believe that they are back in Ancient Rome during the rule of an Etruscan king. The king has decided to build a bridge over the Tiber River and is trying to decide which building company should get the job. Tell students that their group is a building company. Their job is to build an arch that will stand up straight (90 degrees) without breaking apart. (The arch will not be free-standing, but supported on a cardboard surface.)

2. Distribute the arch pattern and materials to each group. Have students transfer the arch pattern to one piece of cardboard by tracing over the pattern heavily in pencil. Then have them darken the lines with the marker and write the numbers EXACTLY as shown on the pattern. This will help make sure the pieces are placed back on the arch in the correct sequence.

3. Have students cut out the arch pieces.

4. Have students also cut out the arch pattern and glue it so its base is on the edge of the other piece of cardboard. This cardboard will act as a building surface and support for the arch the students will build.

5. Allow time for students to experiment with different ways of building their arch. If time passes without success, you may wish to offer some assistance. The easiest way to build the arch is to tip the building surface back slightly. Then begin building up each side of the arch. Place the center piece in last. It helps if someone holds on to the bottom two pieces so they don't slip while building. Slowly tip the building surface upright.

6. Once a group's arch is built, have a group member use the protractor to measure the angle at which the arch is standing. Have groups keep track of how high they can raise the arch before it falls apart. Maybe their first time they got the arch to stand at 45° before it fell apart. Next time, perhaps the angle will be more or less than before. Have groups alert you when they get their arch to stand at 90°.

7. Discuss your findings together or have groups write about their conclusions. Were you able to reach 90°? Why or why not? Describe the steps for building a successful arch. What is the key for holding the arch up? How did it help to build as a group rather than alone? How do you think the Romans built real arches out of stone?

Build an Etruscan Arch *(cont.)*

Important: Number your cardboard pieces exactly as shown on the pattern.

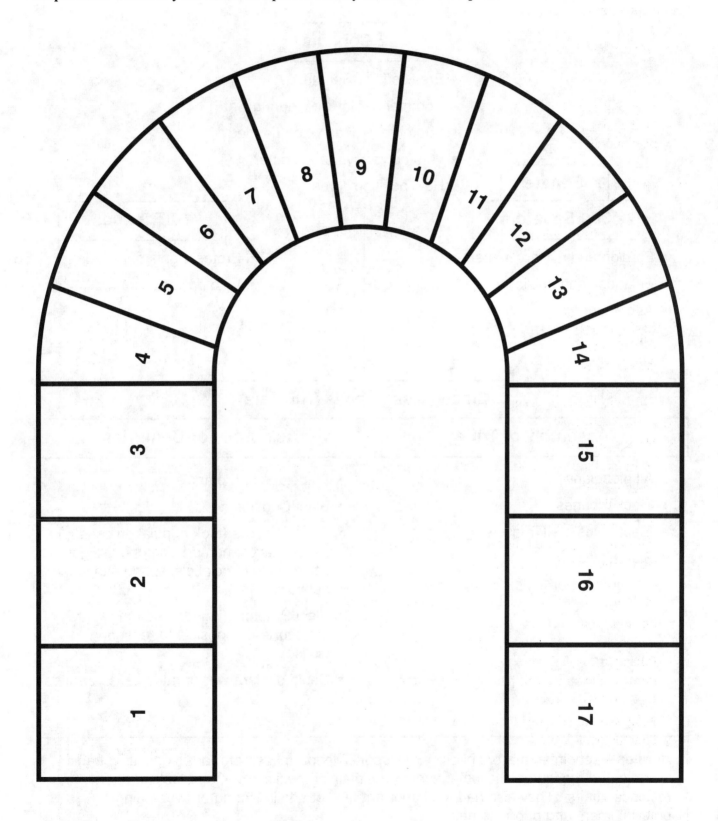

Checks and Balances in the Roman Republic

Make an overhead transparency to use while reading **The Republic and Beyond** (pages 31–34) or provide a copy for students.

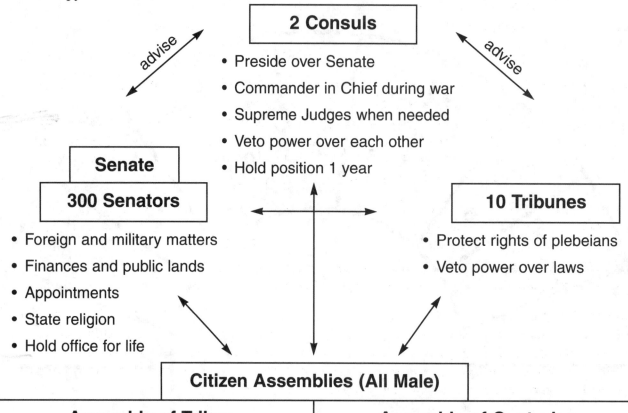

2 Consuls

- Preside over Senate
- Commander in Chief during war
- Supreme Judges when needed
- Veto power over each other
- Hold position 1 year

advise

Senate

300 Senators

- Foreign and military matters
- Finances and public lands
- Appointments
- State religion
- Hold office for life

advise

10 Tribunes

- Protect rights of plebeians
- Veto power over laws

Citizen Assemblies (All Male)

Assembly of Tribes	Assembly of Centuries
• All plebeians	• Plebeians and patricians
• Elect Tribunes	• Elect Consuls
• Elect Questors (Treasurers)	• Elect Censors (took population census), assess taxes, name Senators, assign citizens their social class, and supervise public morals
• Enact laws	• Elect Praetors (judges and magistrates of the courts responsible for ensuring justice)
• Conduct minor trials	• Could declare war or ratify peace treaties

Aediles—appointed mayors of cities. Responsible for upkeep of roads, regulating traffic, weights and measures, the water supply, maintaining public order, and looking after religious affairs. They also had the important task of administering or overseeing entertainment and public games.

The Republic and Beyond

Narrators 1–6	**Pietre**—patrician
Paolo and **Dimitri**—plebeians	**Diedre** and **Flavia**—women
Robustus—middle-class man	**Sentus**—lower-class man
Phoencia—foreigner	**Samson**, **Angelo**, and **Brutus**—slaves

Narrator 1: In 509 B.C., the Romans finally revolted against their Etruscan kings, destroyed the monarchy, and replaced it with a **Republic** in which citizens elected the leaders to run their government. Kings were replaced by two **Consuls**, who were in turn advised by a **Senate** of 300 members. As the Republic evolved, an attempt was made to put together a system of checks and balances, not only between lawmakers and officeholders, but also between the classes of citizens. Join these members of the Republic as they discuss the workings of their government.

Pietre: During this mighty reign of the Republic, the citizens of Rome are divided into two classes: the **patricians** and the **plebeians**. We patricians are a small class of wealthy families that include the Roman nobility. All other citizens are plebeians. The vast majority of these people are peasants, shopkeepers, craftsmen, and small traders. Although most of the plebeians are poor, a number of them have gradually gained wealth, and this has caused changes in our government.

Dimitri: Yes, I am one of the fortunate plebeians to have become wealthy, and I feel it is important that I have the same rights as a patrician. Originally, both patricians and plebeians could vote on matters of the state. However, only patricians could hold important positions in the military, government, or religious sectors. Plebeians had fewer rights than the patricians, yet still had to pay taxes and serve in the army. This did not seem fair.

Narrator 1: By 494 B.C., steps were taken by the plebians to withdraw from Rome and form their own assembly. They were called the **Council of Plebeians**, or **Assembly of Tribes**.

Paolo: We elect our own officials, called **Tribunes**. The wealthy patricians know they cannot survive without their plebeian workforce, so they have negotiated. They allow us to keep our council and leaders. The Tribunes will help protect our plebeian rights, and we can vote against laws we feel are unjust. One of our first victories was to help reform laws and have them written down on 12 bronze plates called **The Twelve Tablets**.

Narrator 1: **The Twelve Tablets** were written in 450 B.C., and the laws were displayed in the Forum for all to see. No longer could a patrician judge interpret the law in any way he saw fit.

The Republic and Beyond *(cont.)*

Narrator 2: Plebians also gained more rights in the 300s B.C. A plebeian could be elected a member of the Senate, and one of the Consuls had to be a plebeian. Debt bondage was outlawed, and even the priesthood was opened to them. By 330 B.C. plebians could even be elected to the official positions of Aedile, Censor, and Praetor.

Dimitri: Despite having plebians elected to official positions, we still had separate political bodies. The laws passed by the predominantly patrician Senate applied to everyone. The laws passed by our plebeian assembly, however, only applied to plebeians. Eventually we had to demand that our laws be applied to everyone.

Narrator 2: In 287 B.C., the patricians finally gave in.

Paolo: We are happy to say that now, after 200 years of struggle, plebeians and patricians are equal under Roman law!

Narrator 2: Were the plebians and the patricians really considered equal? Although the Republic was supposedly balanced by a patrician and a plebeian Consul, the plebeian Tribunes, and other citizen assemblies, the Senate of 300 members was still mostly patrician and the most powerful group in the government. It was the Senate that controlled all foreign policy, the treasury, land holdings, and the state religion.

Narrator 3: The Consuls did have power, but they were limited by design. A Consul was elected for only one year and each Consul could **veto** the other Consul's action. (The word "veto" is from the Latin word meaning "I forbid.") Senators were elected for life. In order for more plebeians to be elected to the Senate, they literally needed to wait for someone to die. Matters were different for the women and the slaves.

Diedre: Women of the Republic are considered citizens. We are protected by the law and enjoy many freedoms that women in other regions are not allowed. A woman in Rome adopts the social class of her husband, and women can own land and their own businesses. But women are not active in the government. We cannot vote or hold office. However, we are able to have a voice in the government by discussing matters with our husbands and attempting to influence their decisions. We are lucky to be given this privilege; in most cultures the woman is not privy to such information.

The Republic and Beyond *(cont.)*

Samson: Women may not have as many rights as men, but we slaves are not even considered citizens. Therefore we have no rights at all. However, life in Rome is not necessarily harsh for all slaves; conditions vary widely. Most slaves work on the estates or in the homes of wealthy families. Trained slaves also work in mining, shipping, and the construction of roads and buildings. Servants are either slaves or ex-slaves. In our system we slaves can be set free, or buy our freedom.

Angelo: For example, many Greeks are brought over to educate the youth in wealthy homes. These slaves are often considered "friends" and freed by their owners, although they continue to serve their former master. Some slaves are even treated as part of the family and not only freed, but adopted as heirs to estates, or may marry into the family.

Samson: Angelo and I are fortunate to work in the home of a kind, wealthy family. The slaves who work in the fields have a much harder life. Of course, we, like all slaves, are always at the mercy of our masters, who have the right to beat or torture us.

Narrator 4: Even when the Republic came to an end in 27 B.C. and Augustus Caesar became the first **emperor**, the social classes in the Empire remained the same, and some strides made by the middle-class during the Republic were lost. As a long string of emperors ruled over the growing Empire, many things remained the same.

Flavia: I feel fortunate to have married a man of wealth and power, for it is only those men in the upper class of Rome that can be appointed by the emperor to positions as government officials. Other jobs acceptable for men in the upper class are jobs in law and farm ownership. Although our elite upper class only makes up about two percent of the population, we are the most powerful and enjoy special legal rights.

Narrator 5: Developing new ideas in law were some of the most lasting contributions of Ancient Rome. The Romans developed case law, in which individual cases are tried and judged based on changing public opinion. They also appointed a well-defined class of legal experts consisting of judges and lawyers. They carried out civil and criminal lawsuits and codified the laws in a series of written volumes. Roman law civilized the world because wherever the Romans conquered, they took their legal concepts with them. Many of the Roman concepts regarding law are still used today in much of the world. Some of these are the use of a professional lawyer, the rules of evidence, the rights of defendants, the use of legal precedents, and the concept that one is innocent until proven guilty.

The Republic and Beyond *(cont.)*

Robustus: Those of us in the middle and lower classes are the ordinary citizens of Rome. We are the farmers, laborers, soldiers, traders, and shopkeepers who do most of the work that sustains the Empire. Unlike in the days when Rome was ruled by the Republic, our status is determined by both birth and wealth. Therefore, people are occasionally able to improve their social status by gaining wealth.

Sentus: This is true, but highly unlikely, for it is very difficult to greatly improve one's income. Most of us work on farms and are lucky to just scrape by each year. A soldier may get a promotion and gain status during his military career, and a woman or man might "marry-up." But it is rare that marriages are arranged outside one's social class.

Robustus: We plebeians actually lost privileges when we began the era of rule by emperors. Laws and punishments vary depending on our social class.

Brutus: Life has changed little for us slaves. We still have no legal rights but do have a chance to better ourselves and possibly be freed by our masters. Some estimate that slaves comprise as much as one-third of the Empire at this time. Although some people complain about slavery, most see it as a necessary part of the workforce.

Phoencia: I do not see how anyone can complain! What other government in the world is willing to give full citizenship and protection to foreigners? I feel privileged to consider myself a Roman and am willing to make the few concessions needed to gain citizenship. This includes speaking Latin, the official language of Rome, worshipping in the manner the emperor chooses, and paying taxes. For some these are great sacrifices, but I don't mind, because I am also allowed to worship in my way and speak my native tongue. You may say I am now a citizen of two lands!

Narrator 6: As the government evolved, more and more people of Rome left the business of running the government to corrupt and greedy upper-class men, thus weakening it. With so many slaves, foreigners, and other factors combined, Rome could not maintain its government. In A.D. 1543, the Turks invaded and caused the fall of the great Roman Empire.

Vocabulary and Comprehension

Write the following words on the chalkboard for students to copy into their vocabulary books. Remind students to define and illustrate each word.

patricians	plebeians
Senate	Consuls
Republic	The Twelve Tablets
veto	Tribunes
Council of Plebeians	emperor

Use all or some of the following questions for whole-class discussion, small-group work, or individual assessment. Allow students to refer back to the story while working.

1. Who controlled the majority of the decision making in the Republic? Why? (*The Senate, because they had the most power over foreign policy, the treasury, land holdings, and religion.*)

2. Do you feel the Republic form of government was fair for all people? Why or why not? (*Accept reasonable answers.*)

3. After the collapse of the Republic and the emergence of ruling emperors, what rights were lost by the middle and lower classes? (*They could no longer hold government offices, and laws and punishments varied depending on one's social class.*)

4. What were some Roman contributions to law? (*use of professional lawyers, rules of evidence, rights of defendants, use of legal precedents, and the concept that one is innocent until proven guilty*)

5. During the reign of the emperors, how could someone improve or lose his or her social status? (*Status depended on wealth and birth. By gaining or losing wealth you could change status.*)

6. How could a foreigner become a citizen? Do you think it was wise to give full citizenship to so many foreigners? Why or why not? (*If a foreigner spoke Latin, paid taxes, and worshipped in the manner designated by the Emperor, he/she could gain citizenship. Accept reasonable answers for the second part.*)

The Rights of the People

Fill in the boxes with the appropriate term: women, patricians, slaves, plebeians.

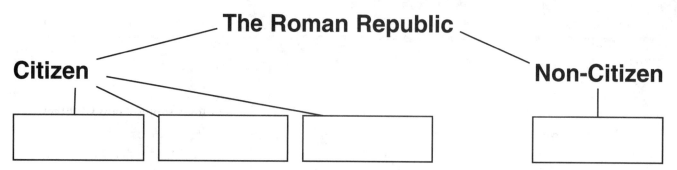

The Roman Republic

Citizen

Non-Citizen

Use the chart below to summarize the rights of the Roman population.

X = Had the right when the Republic was formed

✓ = Gained the right during changes in the Republic

∗ = Lost the right during the reign of the emperors

	Patricians	Plebeians	Women	Slaves
Protected by law				
Equal under the law regardless of social class				
Allowed to vote				
Allowed to own property				
Able to hold a high government office				
Controlled most power				

Read the following quotes and answer the questions in complete sentences on the back of this paper.

1. "Those who know how to win are much more numerous than those who know how to make proper use of their victories." (Polybius, 2nd century B.C.) What do you think Polybius means by this quote? How did the Romans apply this concept to their idea of government and leadership?

2. "Intelligence, and reflection, and judgment reside in old men, and if there had been none of them, no states could exist at all." (Cicero, 106–43 B.C.) How is this philosophy demonstrated by the Roman government? Do we use this same philosophy today when choosing our leaders?

Comparison Writing:
The Republic vs. Democracy

Have students relate the Roman government to their own lives by writing a comparison composition. Keep in mind that you can use this lesson format for other assignments appropriate for comparison writing.

Preparing for the lesson:

1. Make overhead transparencies of the Writing Process (page 39) and the Compare and Contrast Chart (page 41).

2. Reproduce an Editing Checklist (page 40) and a Compare and Contrast Chart (page 41) for each student.

3. Write the Words that Compare and Contrast (page 38) on the chalkboard.

Teaching the lesson:

1. Tell students that they are going to write a composition comparing the Roman Republic to their own form of government, a democracy. Provide materials for the class to use that present information about a republic and a democracy, and specifically the Roman Republic and American democracy.

2. Using the overhead transparency, review the Writing Process. Then distribute a copy of the Compare and Contrast Chart to each student. Tell students to use this form for the prewriting stage of their composition.

3. Display the overhead transparency of the Compare and Contrast Chart. Have students write "Roman Republic" in the space for Subject #1 and "Democracy" for Subject #2. Brainstorm with the class some categories for comparing/contrasting (gaining citizenship, rights of people, voting, leaders and offices, how decisions are made, etc.). Have students choose at least four of these categories and list them in the center column on their chart.

4. Discuss with the students the steps for using the Compare and Contrast Chart to help write their compositions.

   a. The **introduction** should give the reader some interesting background that will make him or her want to read the rest of the composition. The introduction should also let the reader know the name of the two subjects being compared (Roman Republic and American democracy).

   b. The **supporting details** will be found in the students' research. Remind students that they should include as many details as possible in their compositions.

   c. The **conclusion** should restate the names of the two subjects (Roman Republic and Democracy), give a short summary that describes what the composition was about, and provide closing remarks.

5. Tell students to compare/contrast each category in a separate paragraph. Each paragraph should open with a sentence describing the category and include all of the supporting details for one subject (Roman Republic), and then all of the supporting details for the other subject (democracy).

The Republic vs. Democracy *(cont.)*

6. Review with students the Words that Compare and Contrast and encourage them to use a variety of words in their compositions.

Words that Compare

same	much
similar	like
also	as well as
alike	similarly
in common	likewise
each	both
too	

Words that Contrast

differ	on the other hand
different	yet
differently	although
differences	but
however	unlike

7. Have students follow the Writing Process as they write their compositions.

8. Distribute and review the Editing Checklist to remind students of the steps needed to improve their rough drafts. The first editor should "listen" to the composition to help revise aspects such as incorrect sentence structure, incorrect sequence, unclear information, insufficient details, etc.

9. Students should make the first revisions and then ask a second editor to read the composition and look for mechanical errors such as spelling and punctuation, as well as checking the content.

10. Have students write their final drafts after editing. Once completed, have students share their compositions with the class. You may wish to choose a few examples to display in the classroom.

The Writing Process

PREWRITE

Cluster, outline, brainstorm, draw, and discuss your ideas. Then make a plan to organize your ideas.

↓

FIRST DRAFT WRITING

Write down your ideas. Skip every other line. Use the information you recorded on your prewriting plan to organize your ideas in a logical manner. Do not worry about spelling, capitalization, punctuation, or grammar. Read over your first draft to be sure it makes sense.

↓

RESPONSE

Read your composition to a partner and get feedback to help clarify ideas. Have your partner help you identify the strengths and improve the weaknesses in your composition.

↓

REVISION

Add details and descriptive words or phrases to your composition. You may need to change the sequence of sentences in order to clarify the ideas.

↓

EDITING AND REWRITING

Have a second partner read your composition and help you make any grammatical and mechanical (spelling, capitalization, punctuation) corrections.

↓

EVALUATION

Be sure you and your partners use the Editing Checklist to evaluate your composition.

↓

PUBLISHING

Type or use your best handwriting to recopy your composition. Check it over again before turning it in to the teacher.

Editing Checklist

Name _____

Title _____

X = No changes needed   ✔ = Just okay   ✱ = Problem. Editor will help make corrections.

	1st Editor Listen and revise	2nd Editor Read and revise	Teacher Comments
Proper format? (introduction, supporting details, conclusion)			
Specific supporting details? (Use of metaphors, figurative language, similes, descriptions, examples, adjectives, adverbs, prepositional phrases, etc.)			
Correct sentence structure, grammar, and word use?			
Correct spelling?			
Correct punctuation? (periods, commas, quotation marks)			
Correct capitalization? (proper nouns, sentence beginnings)			
Strengths of composition?			
Weaknesses of composition? (editors help make corrections)			

_____   _____
1st Editor   2nd Editor

Compare and Contrast Chart

Introduction:		

Subject #1		Subject #2
Supporting Details	Categories	Supporting Details

Conclusion:	

The Punic Wars

By 270 B.C. the Romans had conquered the entire Italian peninsula and began looking outward for expansion. Some countries in the Mediterranean region accepted Roman domination, while others resisted. At this time there was also another great power in the Mediterranean offering competition—Carthage, a region on the North African coast that had been settled by Phoenicians who came from Syria. Carthage had become a great seafaring nation and led the area in trading. Carthage also had settlements on the islands of Sicily and Sardinia, as well as some settlements along the coast of Spain. It was inevitable that these two great powers would someday come into conflict.

The ongoing battle between the Roman Republic and Carthage over the right to rule the Mediterranean took the form of three major wars known as the Punic Wars. "Punic" is Latin for "Carthaginian." In 264 B.C. the Roman Republic broke an earlier alliance with Carthage and invaded Sicily. This caused the First Punic War. The Republic did well on land but suffered many defeats at sea. But the Romans learned quickly and soon developed a more efficient navy. The ships from Carthage were built to ram the enemy. To better defend against them, the Romans built ships designed to hook onto the sides of the Carthaginian ships to fight, rather than face the enemy head on.

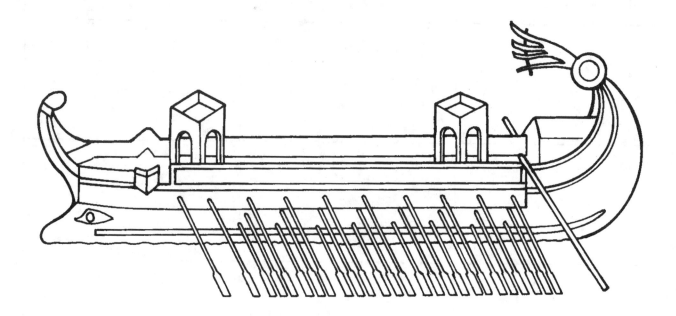

Many times the Romans were rebuffed, but they forged ahead, expanding their fleet to 200 ships. Finally, at the battle of Aegates, they won a great victory and began their march into the Mediterranean. They captured the islands of Sicily, Sardinia, and Corsica in 225 B.C. These islands were strategic trading posts for the Carthaginians and therefore great losses for them.

Now the Carthaginians had to look elsewhere to form their trading center, and they chose Spain. General Hamilcar Barca quickly expanded control over a large area of Spain using their already established trading posts. Spain proved to be a wise conquest for Carthage. Not only did it supply fish and many other needed foods, but it also contained rich deposits of copper, iron, and silver. Unfortunately, Hamilcar was killed in battle while expanding land holdings. In 221 B.C. his son, Hannibal, was elected commander. Hannibal had been raised by his father to be a sworn enemy of the Roman Republic . Although he was only 26 years old, it was time for him to fulfill his destiny.

The Punic Wars *(cont.)*

Rome looked on anxiously as Carthage expanded throughout Spain. Then, in 219 B.C., Hannibal and his troops attacked Saguntum, an ally of Rome. The fall of Saguntum marked the beginning of the Second Punic War. This time the disputed territory was Spain. As Rome sent troops to the west, Hannibal planned a surprise invasion of Italy from the north. He gathered a force of 60,000 soldiers, 6,000 horses, and 37 elephants. He felt his advance by land was the last thing the Romans would expect, because the route from Spain over the Alps was difficult and dangerous.

The long march began in Spain and moved across the south of Gaul (France). One of Hannibal's first problems was to get his army across a wide river. Big rafts were built to ferry the elephants across. Five months later he reached the Alps, which were covered in snow and ice. Only half of his original army remained, but this did not deter Hannibal.

The main passes through the Alps were guarded by the Romans, so Hannibal chose a narrow twisting route instead. His elephants acted as battering rams when he needed to crush through deep snow. Many men and animals died on the journey. Once Hannibal reached Italy, he began recruiting more men. He rebuilt his army, then moved quickly through Italy, enjoying victory after victory until he reached the very walls of Rome itself. Once there, he did not have enough supplies for a siege, and he saw that the walls could not be breached.

Meanwhile, the Romans knew they had to try something different with Hannibal. Instead of meeting him head-on in battle, they decided to lead him on a wild goose chase, keeping his army just outside striking distance. This tactic worked. Hannibal pursued the Roman army over much of Italy without really engaging them in battle. This gave the Republic time to recruit more soldiers and caused the Carthaginians to run low on supplies.

The Punic Wars *(cont.)*

Still Hannibal was invincible in Italy, although the Roman Republic defeated the Carthaginians everywhere else. The Romans now had a brilliant general named Scipio. He conquered Spain for Rome and turned his attention to North Africa. After 14 years in Italy, Hannibal was forced to return home to defend his homeland.

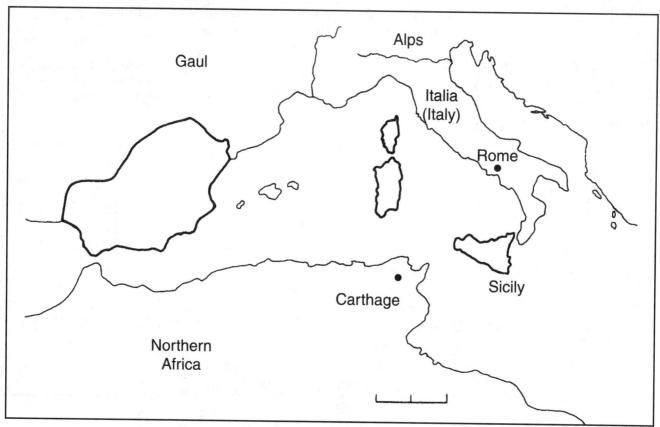

These two powerful generals had great respect for one another. They agreed to meet and talk before the planned battle at Zama near Carthage. Hannibal asked for a private interview with Scipio, to be held in an open area between the two armies. Although they had known of each other for over 15 years, this was the first time they had met face to face. Using interpreters, they spoke together at great length. Still, the fight began.

Miraculously, both great leaders survived Zama. However, Hannibal was defeated and Carthage was forced to give up Spain. The peace terms put forward by Scipio allowed Carthage to keep its own lands. Hannibal escaped to the Middle East, but some years later the Romans demanded his surrender. Rather than face captivity in Rome, Hannibal, then 65 years old, committed suicide by poison.

Peace existed between Rome and Carthage for some years. However, many Romans still felt threatened as long as Carthage existed. When Carthage again rebelled, the Roman army destroyed the city once and for all in the Third Punic War. The surviving Carthaginians were sold into slavery, and North Africa became part of the growing Roman Empire.

With the final defeat of Carthage, Rome was now the most powerful force in the western Mediterranean. Rome turned eastward and began its further conquest with Greece and Macedonia. By 50 B.C. the Roman Republic was in control of the entire Mediterranean region and well on its way to becoming a mighty empire.

44

Cause and Effect

Have students use the information from The Punic Wars (pages 42–44) to make a chart showing the cause and effect of each of the Punic Wars. An example is shown below.

	Cause	Effect
First Punic War	Rome breaks alliance with Carthage and invades Sicily	Rome prevails and captures Sicily, Sardinia, and Corsica
Second Punic War	Carthage conquers Spain, Hannibal invades Italy	Rome defeats Hannibal but Carthage allowed to keep its lands
Third Punic War	Carthage rebels against Roman rule	Rome completely destroys Carthage

The Punic Debates

Tell the class they will try to prevent the Third Punic War. Divide the class into two teams, and have each team represent their team's general—Carthage (Hannibal) and Rome (Scipio). Allow time for teams to research and develop points each man would have presented during their talk before the battle at Zama. Each side will try to convince the other that their side should be allowed to rule Carthage and North Africa.

Assign a team leader to make sure each member of the group participates in research and discussion. Choose a timekeeper who will limit each speaker to two minutes to give his or her point or rebuttal. Set up tables across from each other to hold the debate.

Since Hannibal called the meeting, allow a Roman to begin the talks. After one team member presents a point for Rome, allow a Carthaginian to rebut the point. Then have a different Carthaginian present a point for Carthage, and a different Roman rebut the point. Alternate this pro/con format until the teams resolve whether or not to go to war again.

Discuss with the class whether or not this type of negotiation could work in a major conflict. What are the advantages of negotiation? Why would preventing a war perhaps be more important to both sides today than during the Punic Wars?

Publish a Newspaper

Write articles and create graphics to make a class newspaper giving facts and opinions about the Punic Wars. Combine the sections to make a class newspaper. Here are some suggestions to get you started.

- Current Events—battles, cause and effect of the wars, wartime tragedies
- Obituaries—for Hamilcar and Hannibal
- Classified Ads—soldiers, elephants, ship builders, etc.
- Real Estate—homes for sale in Sicily, Carthage, Sardinia
- Weather Forecast—winter in the Alps
- Horoscopes—outlooks for different leaders during the wars
- Business Section—treaties drawn, monies paid, new ships built, etc.
- Dear Hanna—advice to the war torn

Draft a Peace Treaty

When Rome defeated General Hamilcar Barca at Aegates, a treaty defining the terms of peace was drawn up. Rome demanded Carthage pay it 3,200 talents of silver over ten years. All Carthaginians were forced to leave Sicily and give up all claim to it. Carthage also had to return all Italian prisoners of war and keep their ships out of Roman waters. Finally, Carthage had to agree that they would never attack cities that were allies of Rome.

Imagine that you are the Roman leader in charge of drawing up the peace treaty to end a Punic War. You are the victor, so you must be clear in defining what you want from Carthage. Use the following words in your treaty:

hostilities	– fighting or warfare
conflict	– struggle or battle
reparation	– compensation in money or goods that is paid by a defeated nation to the victor for damages and injury caused by the war.
disputed territory	– the land or region over which the war is fought
defeat	– to win a victory over
repatriate	– to send people back to their own nation

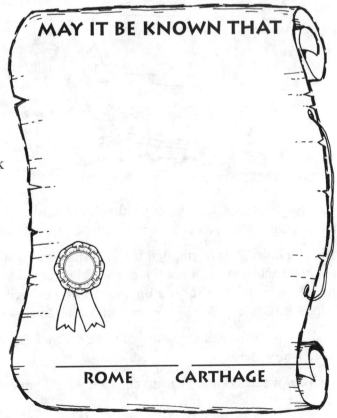

MAY IT BE KNOWN THAT

ROME   CARTHAGE

Write your treaty on manila paper using black pen. Sign the treaty for yourself and the defeated general. Tear the edges of the document to make it look old, and roll it into a scroll tied with ribbon. You may wish to include a picture of an official seal.

You Were There

Historians have learned a great deal about actual events in ancient times through journals that people made. The more detailed the journals, the more we are able to learn about life in other ages.

Imagine that you are a soldier who fought in one of the Punic Wars. Use construction paper and writing paper to make a journal in which you record your feelings and thoughts and the things you have seen. Use the suggestions below to guide your research and your journal entries.

1. Are you fighting for Rome or Carthage? Describe what it is like being in this army or navy, tell about your leaders, and describe the physical conditions you must endure.

2. Which Punic War are you fighting in? Make sure you write about one particular war. These could be actual events or fictional events that could have happened, based on information you found. Are you on a ship during the invasion of Sicily? Are you with Hannibal as he crosses the Alps with the elephants? Are you part of the final destruction of Carthage?

3. Make at least five dated journal entries. Write them so a reader would feel as though he or she were really there.

4. Include pictures or diagrams to enhance your journal entries.

Julius Caesar

Narrators 1–5

Samuel and **Oxaviar**—soldiers

Alexandra, Justin, and **Flaudine**—citizens

Claudia and **Jermane**—plebeians

Marthinian and **Daledus**—senators

Narrator 1: From 509 B.C. to 50 B.C., Rome was a republic. Although no longer ruled by kings, it still was not very democratic. Most of the power was in the hands of the Senate, who were patrician men. For years the plebeians fought for more rights. Although they made some progress, power was never equally shared by the two classes.

Narrator 2: Around 50 B.C. a powerful Roman general named **Julius Caesar** took control of the Republic and declared himself **dictator**. He rendered the Senate helpless, and many believed his ambition would lead him to declare himself king of Rome and form a dynasty of rulers. In order to preserve the Roman Republic, a group of men assassinated Caesar. Join a group of Roman citizens on March 15, 44 B.C. in the Forum as they learn of Caesar's death and recount his incredible life.

Justin: Have you heard? Have you heard? Julius Caesar was just assassinated on the steps of the Senate! Caesar had been warned by his fortuneteller of danger, but he disregarded the warnings and dismissed his bodyguards. As he approached the Senate, a man pulled back his robe. This was the signal to attack. A horde of men with daggers lunged at him. Rumor has it he was stabbed more than 23 times.

Alexandra: How horrible to suffer such a death, but I can't say he didn't have it coming to him. Such a pity that a man with so fine an upbringing could let his ambition get the best of him. He was born into a fine patrician family. His wealth and education prepared him for the high positions the aristocracy fills in Roman society. By the time he was 20, he was serving in the army and anticipating moving into the higher ranks.

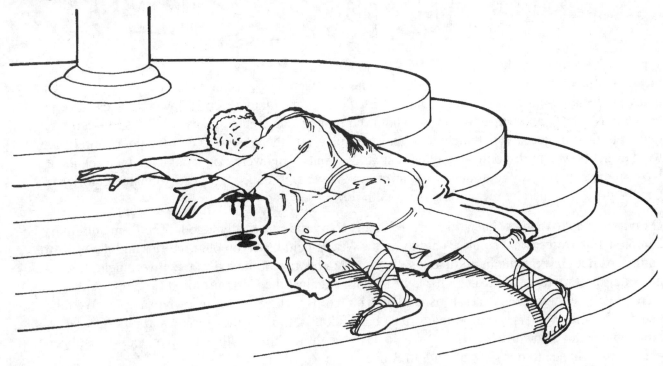

Julius Caesar (cont.)

Samuel: And no better soldier could you find. Although he was very proud and vain, he was also a brave fighter and steady leader. One legend tells of how Caesar was captured by pirates while still a young soldier. They could tell he was from a high-class family so they demanded a ransom. Caesar laughed, saying they obviously did not know who they had, and he himself increased the ransom to an amount worthy of his status. Caesar sent one of his companions to raise the money while he stayed with the pirates. He told them that he would return someday to recover the money and punish their deed. The pirates thought this all a big joke and released him once the money arrived. To their dismay, Caesar did return with a fleet of ships and took revenge. Ah, yes, such a pity to have a man like that killed.

Claudia: I know you think he was a disgraceful ruler, Alexandra, yet I must agree with Samuel and mourn at his loss. Julius Caesar has done more to help us plebeians than any other Roman. Although he was rich, he was always fighting for the poor. After serving as a soldier, Caesar began his career in the government.

Jermane: I remember the time he threw a great party for 20,000 poor people. He gave away money, bread, and precious oil for lamps. I understand he was even more generous to his soldiers. It is said many were paid with rich farmland. During his rule he made many reforms, lowered taxes, gave jobs to veterans of war, and helped out those who owed money. He created many new jobs through his many building projects, which included canals, temples, and theaters. Some of the poorest in Rome were even allowed to discontinue paying rent at all. And if this were not enough, he then set about to prove himself worthy by returning to the military. As general, he led our army to many victories in Gaul and Britain, thereby regaining great wealth for himself and Rome.

Oxaviar: Yes, to many soldiers like myself Julius Caesar is practically a god. The Roman military is comprised of professional soldiers paid to fight. We are paid based on our victories and the spoils of battle. Although some might not like the way Caesar conducted himself in the government, there was no better military leader in Rome. I fought with him against the Germans hired by Gaul. Although we were greatly outnumbered, Caesar inspired us with words and led us by his own example. We felt we had superhuman powers. The Germans must have felt this, too, for they turned and ran! Caesar was quite a man and a powerful general. I would have fought for him anytime or anyplace. We soldiers pledge our alliance to our generals, not to Rome or the Republic.

Julius Caesar (cont.)

Marthinian: And because of this, greedy and power-hungry generals have fought one another for power in the government. I know that most Romans like yourselves approved of Julius Caesar's conquests, but some of us were wary of his growing power and influence. Pompey, a rival general and once a friend of Caesar's, was the most distrusting. He convinced many of us Senators that Caesar was plotting against the government. The Senate declared Caesar a public enemy and ordered him to disband his army. Caesar attempted to compromise, but Pompey refused each compromise he offered. Things would have been different for Caesar and Rome had he chosen to follow our orders.

Narrator 3: It was in 49 B.C. that Julius Caesar made the most important decision of his life. While his army stood beside the **Rubicon River** bordering Italy, he pondered his choices. If he crossed into Italy with his men it would surely mean civil war, for he would be blatantly ignoring the Senate's orders. Furthermore, it was considered treason for a general to leave his own province and bring his army to Rome. However, if he stayed, he would be without an army, power, or hope. Allowing his ambition to guide his decision, Julius Caesar ordered his men to march across the bridge, thereby declaring war against the Roman Republic.

Narrator 4: Pompey and the Senate fought Caesar, and although they had the larger army, they were not as well organized. Pompey's army hadn't fought a major war for years and thus was unprepared for the hardened and loyal soldiers fighting for Caesar. The battles extended into Greece, at which time Pompey fled to Egypt, where he was eventually murdered. Julius Caesar declared himself leader of Rome, in control of the armies and the Senate.

Daledus: Yes, we could have avoided this ugly mess had Julius Caesar followed our orders back at the Rubicon. Once he came to Rome his ambition got the best of him, and he had to be stopped. Jermane, you think he cared about the common people, but he just bought your support by handing out bread and providing you with entertainment. The only thing Julius Caesar ever really cared about was power and control. Sure, we in the Senate voted to make him dictator. But what else could we do? His popularity among the citizens and military rendered us helpless to do otherwise. Once dictator, there was no end to his lust for power.

Julius Caesar *(cont.)*

Flaudine: I heard that he treated the Senators as if they were common beggars. He thought himself so above others that he had a special chair made and layered with gold. He would sit on this "throne" while presiding over meetings. The other Senators also resented the fact that he refused to stand when speaking with them. We all saw the coins minted with his profile and that grand statue made from ivory that was paraded around the city. Dictators are usually voted in as a temporary measure. Caesar was not interested in losing his status, so I can't help but think he was attempting to make himself a permanent ruler and possibly king.

Marthinian: He was gaining more and more land for Rome, but it was questionable who his alliance was really with. Once he conquered Egypt and became involved with **Queen Cleopatra**, he only grew more and more greedy for power. I'm sure she was a guiding force behind his ambition, hoping to gain power for herself as well. Many believed he intended to found a dynasty with himself the first king. Then he would get rid of the Senate and there would be no more voting by the people. I tell you, he had to be stopped.

Justin: Sorry to interrupt, my friends, but I have more details about the murder. Cassius and Brutus were involved in the assassination plot. Can you believe it? Brutus was one of Caesar's best friends! Many believe he may even be Caesar's natural son. So you can imagine Caesar's shock when he saw Brutus approach with dagger raised. They say Caesar actually stopped resisting when he saw Brutus and sadly cried, "Et tu, Brute?" The Forum is buzzing with excitement. Mobs are forming to track down the assassins. Rome is divided and I fear the fate of our fair city.

Narrator 5: The assassination of Julius Caesar hurt the Republic further rather than saved it. Rome became divided, and a terrible power struggle followed. Caesar's adopted son Octavian returned to Rome after hearing of his father's murder. Octavian assumed partial control of the Roman Empire and later became its first emperor, thus putting an end to the Roman Republic.

Vocabulary and Comprehension

Write the following words on the chalkboard for students to copy into their vocabulary books. Remind students to define and illustrate each word.

Julius Caesar	**dictator**	**Rubicon River**	**Queen Cleopatra**

Use all or some of the following questions for whole-class discussion, small-group work, or individual assessment. Allow students to refer back to the story while working.

1. List the major events in Julius Caesar's life that helped make him dictator of Rome. (*Julius Caesar was very ambitious and planned his life accordingly. He joined the army and, after being a successful soldier, he worked in the government. After he gained great popularity with the general public, he went back into the military to gain more glory and money. He became a very wealthy and popular general and was successful in gaining land for Rome. Some felt he was becoming too powerful and not acting on behalf of the Republic. The Senate ordered him to disband his army, but instead he marched over the Rubicon and began a civil war. Once he won the war, the Senate voted him dictator.*)

2. Why was the crossing of the Rubicon such a big decision for Caesar? Do you feel he made the right decision? Why or why not? (*Julius Caesar knew that his decision would determine his future. By crossing the Rubicon he would either gain more power or possibly be killed. Accept reasonable answers for the other parts.*)

3. Why was Julius Caesar popular with the majority of plebeians and soldiers? (*He spent money on entertaining the people, he created jobs, he made tax reforms, and he paid his soldiers well with spoils and land.*)

4. Why did the Senate dislike Caesar? (*He became too powerful. He began acting more like a king than the head of the Republic. The Senate feared he would use his popularity with the people to make himself king and begin a dynasty.*)

5. Why was Julius Caesar assassinated? (*The people who killed him thought they could save the Republic form of government by getting rid of Julius Caesar and his way of doing things.*)

6. Did the assassination achieve its goal? (*No. Instead of saving the Republic, Caesar's death instead began a series of civil wars.*)

7. How might the history of Rome have been different had Julius Caesar followed the orders of the Senate and disbanded his army? (*Accept reasonable answers.*)

Make a Personal Timeline

Discuss with the class how Julius Caesar accomplished many goals because he was ambitious and determined. He decided what he wanted to do, where he would go, and how he could get there. Careful planning helped him achieve his goals. Of course, nobody can plan for everything, and there are always surprises along the way. Still, setting goals and striving to reach them—even if you must change them along the way—helps you make important decisions about your life.

Invite students to think about their future and their goals. How do they plan to reach these goals? What are the steps they need to follow to get there? Provide strips of construction paper and have students create personal timelines. Have them indicate the age at which they hope to achieve goals such as education, training, working, having a family, retiring, etc. Discuss realistic goals and steps as opposed to idealistic goals. For example, how many people actually become professional athletes? Can you plan to win a lottery? How easy is it to become a famous celebrity?

After students have constructed and described their timelines, discuss how making decisions could change their futures. For example, if they choose to drop out of high school, how will that affect their future? If they decide to do drugs or join a gang, how could that alter the path they have chosen?

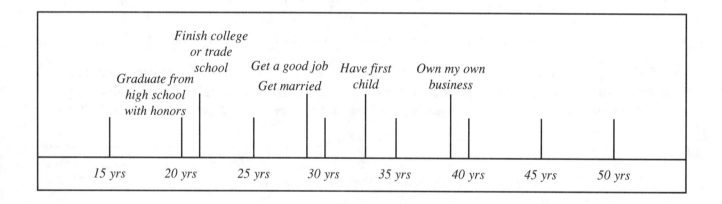

Autobiographical Incident

Reproduce an Autobiographical Incident Organizer (page 55) for each student. Read the prompt together and discuss some major decisions that might have been made by students in their lifetime. Caution students to preserve their privacy and that of their families when they choose an incident. Review with the class the different sections of the composition. Display an overhead transparency of The Writing Process (page 39) for students to use as they write. Give students time to edit their first drafts using the Editing Checklist (page 40) and write their final drafts. Allow volunteers to share their compositions.

Autobiographical Incident Organizer

Crossing the Rubicon

When Julius Caesar made the decision to lead his army across the Rubicon River, he knew his life would forever be changed. Today when someone says they have "crossed the Rubicon," it means they have made an important decision that they won't be able to change and which will affect the rest of their life.

Recall a time in your past in which you made an important decision that has affected your life ever since. It might be choosing a friend; deciding how to spend your money; turning down cigarettes, alcohol, or drugs; or helping to make a family decision. Write about the event and tell why you feel it was a "Rubicon" for you.

Introduction/Opening Statement—The opening statement tells what you are going to write about. You can restate the prompt and add your event, or start with an action from your story.

_____

_____

_____

_____

_____

Specific Supporting Details/Sequence Statements—The body of your composition must include a clear sequence of what happened, the setting of the event, and the reactions and feelings of the characters involved. Jot down a brief sequence of events you can expand in your composition.

1. _____
2. _____
3. _____
4. _____
5. _____

Conclusion/Summary Statement—Summarize the decision you made, say whether or not you're glad you made it, and tell why it was your "Rubicon." Write a strong closing sentence.

_____

_____

_____

_____

Give a Persuasive Speech

Enhance and assess your students' ability to use oral language effectively to persuade.

Preparing for the lesson:

1. Reproduce a Persuasive Speech Organizer (page 57) for each student.

2. Create an overhead transparency of the Speech Evaluation Form (page 58) and reproduce one for each student. You will use these to record your evaluation of each student's speech.

3. Schedule approximately 30–45 minutes during each of three days for 8–10 students to give their speeches.

Teaching the lesson:

1. Discuss with students the importance of being a persuasive speaker. Remind students that Julius Caesar's life and the fate of the Roman Republic could have been different had participants been persuaded to act or think a different way. Explain that they will have an opportunity to go back in history and try to persuade others to take certain action for or against Julius Caesar.

2. Divide the class into the following groups A–F.

   A. You are Pompey. Persuade the Senate to stop Caesar.

   B. You are a plebeian citizen. Persuade the Senate to ignore Pompey.

   C. You are a Senator. Persuade Caesar to disband his army.

   D. You are Caesar. Persuade your army to disregard the Senate's order.

   E. You are Brutus. Persuade the Senate to assassinate Caesar.

   F. You are Mark Antony. Persuade the Senate to spare the life of Caesar.

3. Have each group research to find information that will help their speech. Allow students to work together to gather information, but tell them each person will give his or her own speech.

4. Distribute a Persuasive Speech Organizer to each student. Review it with students to help them better organize their speeches.

5. Using the overhead transparency, review the Speech Evaluation Form so that students know what is expected of them during their speeches.

6. Assign each pair of groups a speaking date. Day 1, groups A and B; Day 2, groups C and D; Day 3, groups E and F.

7. Evaluate the individual speeches using the Speech Evaluation Form.

8. After each set of speeches, have the class vote whether or not they would have made the same decision the Romans did. Discuss why students were persuaded and how history might have been different had the decisions been different.

Persuasive Speech Organizer

Introduction (Tell background information, the issue, your position on the issue, and three main reasons for your position.) _____

_____

_____

Reason #1	Supporting Details
Reason #2	Supporting Details
Reason #3	Supporting Details

Conclusion (Summarize your reasons; give a convincing closing statement.) _____

_____

_____

_____

_____

Speech Evaluation Form

Speaker _____

> **X** = No changes needed   ✔ = Just okay   ✷ = Problem. Editor will help make corrections.

Place an evaluation mark in each category, along with some constructive comments.

Speech Format:

❏ Introduction (background to gain interest) _____

❏ Body (specific supporting details)_____

❏ Conclusion (summary and closing statement)_____

Speaking Technique:

❏ Voice Expression (volume, speed, and inflection) _____

❏ Sentence Structure (clear and complete sentences, without run-ons)_____

❏ Correct Grammar_____

❏ Eye Contact (look at audience) _____

❏ Appropriate Hand Gestures _____

❏ Visual Aids (props, pictures) _____

❏ Prepared and Rehearsed (smooth delivery)_____

❏ Time Limit (3–5 minutes) _____

Best part of the speech? _____

_____

_____

_____

Suggestions for improvement? _____

_____

_____

_____

Evaluator_____

Julius Caesar, Mark Antony, and Cleopatra

Character Search: The story of Julius Caesar's life has a confusing cast of characters. Have a group of students research and report back to the class the relationship among these people: Julius Caesar, Octavian, Mark Antony, Cleopatra, Brutus.

Suggested formats for the reports are a talk show, news broadcast, play, or other reenactment. Have students create a visual aid to show the characters and describe their relationship to each other.

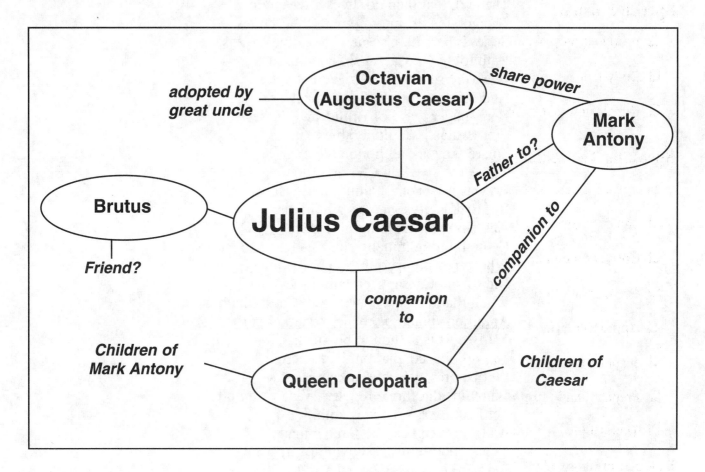

***Cleopatra*, The Movie:** Another fun way to help students better understand the relationship of these characters is to watch the classic Elizabeth Taylor version of *Cleopatra*. The movie is about two hours long, so you may prefer to present it on two different days. Be sure to preview the movie and make note of areas in which you want to stimulate class discussion. Remind students that this is a Hollywood production and therefore not completely authentic.

Biography Reports: Have students research the participants in Julius Caesar's life and write a brief biography on the one they find most interesting. Have students illustrate their person, and display their biographies and pictures in the classroom.

Mark Antony Speaks

Below is an oration given by Mark Antony at the Forum in Rome. This speech is taken from Act III, Scene II in the famous play *Julius Caesar* by William Shakespeare. Discuss the meaning of Antony's speech and the meaning of the underlined words or phrases.

Friends, Romans, countrymen, lend me your ears;
I come to bury Caesar, not to praise him.
The evil, that men do, lives after them;
The good is oft interred with their bones;
So let it be with Caesar. The noble Brutus
Hath told you, Caesar was ambitious;
If it were so, it was a grievous fault;
And grievously hath Caesar answer'd it.
Here, under leave of Brutus and the rest
(For Brutus is an honorable man;
So are they all, all honorable men;)
Come I to speak in Caesar's funeral.
He was my friend, faithful and just to me:
But Brutus says, he was ambitious;
And Brutus is an honorable man.
He hath brought many captives home to Rome,
Whose ransoms did the general coffer fill:
Did this in Caesar seem ambitious?
When that the poor have cried, Caesar hath wept;
Ambition should be made of sterner stuff:
Yet Brutus is an honorable man.
You all did see, that on the Lupercal
I thrice presented him a kingly crown,
Which he did thrice refuse. Was this ambition?
Yet Brutus says, he was ambitious;
And, sure, he is an honorable man.
I speak not to disprove what Brutus spoke,
But here I am to speak what I do know.
You all did love him once, not without cause;
What cause withholds you then to mourn for him?
O judgement, thou art fled to brutish beasts
And men have lost their reason!—Bear with me
My heart is in the coffin there with Caesar,
And I must pause till it come back to me.

lend me your ears—listen to me
oft interred—often buried
hath—has
under leave—with permission
Whose ransoms did the general coffer fill—Who got money for Rome by holding captives for ransom?
Ambition should be made of sterner stuff—A truly ambitious person would not be so weak as to cry for the poor, as did Caesar.
thrice—three times
I speak not to disprove what Brutus spoke—I'm not calling Brutus a liar
What cause withholds you then to mourn for him? O judgement, thou art fled to brutish beasts—What makes you not mourn for Caesar? Your good judgment has been overshadowed by bad men.

Octavian/Augustus Caesar

Gaius Octavius was born into a wealthy patrician family in 63 B.C. He had a fairly normal childhood living at his family's country villa and going to school. He was an intelligent and serious-minded youth.

Julius Caesar, his great-uncle, adopted Gaius Octavius and named him his son and heir. The young man then changed his name to Gaius Julius Caesar Octavianus and was known as Caesar Octavian. He was proud of his name and worked hard to impress his new father. When Julius Caesar was murdered in 44 B.C., Octavian was completing his studies in Greece. By the time the news reached him, citizens and soldiers had assembled to pledge him their alliance and support as Caesar's heir. Octavian declined their request to march on Rome and claim his heritage. He chose instead to journey alone and assess the situation.

Upon reaching Rome, he learned of the chaos facing his people. Brutus and Cassius, the leaders of Caesar's assassination, had hoped to restore the Roman Republic, but there was no clear leadership or plan of action. The two men were suspicious of Octavian and his motives when he decided to join the Senate. Octavian had the support of Mark Antony, one of Caesar's closest allies. But since Mark Antony had hoped to be the sole heir of Caesar's growing empire, his support was tainted.

Aware of these suspicions and hostilities, Octavian moved slowly into a position of power. He made friends within the Senate and eventually established himself as an equal of Mark Antony. Working together, they defeated Brutus and Cassius, finally avenging the death of their beloved Caesar and becoming joint rulers of the Roman Empire.

Still, Octavian and Antony had many differences, and soon it was clear that they could not rule the Empire together. They agreed to split the territory in half. Antony, being the older and more experienced of the two, claimed the eastern portion, which was rich and well developed. Octavian ruled the western segment.

Mark Antony decided to rule his half of the Roman Empire from Egypt. Just as Julius Caesar before him had been influenced by Queen Cleopatra's intellect and beauty, so too was Mark Antony. Soon the two of them were ruling together and, at the same time, nurturing a romance that sent shock waves throughout the Empire.

Octavian/Augustus Caesar *(cont.)*

Octavian set about restoring the Western Empire to its former glory. For ten years he worked diligently, gaining the respect of his people. When word reached Rome that Antony intended to divide the Eastern Empire between Cleopatra and their children, Octavian and the Senate declared war on them. Rather than being dragged back to Rome a criminal, Antony retreated to Egypt, where he committed suicide. Heartbroken and humiliated, Queen Cleopatra used an asp, or very poisonous snake, to kill herself.

Octavian now was the sole ruler of the Roman Empire, and peace was declared for the first time in over 15 years. In 27 B.C., the Senate voted to give Octavian a new name—Augustus—meaning "respected," "revered," or "divine." Augustus Caesar ruled until A.D. 14 and was careful not to make the same mistakes as his father.

Julius Caesar had flaunted his power and disrespected the Senate. Augustus knew that the idea of a king was still unpopular, so he appeared to support the Republic and repeatedly suggested he should resign his leadership once the government was fully working. With this tactic he hoped the Senate would ask him to remain sole leader. Augustus also allowed the Senate to control many aspects of the government while he alone controlled the military.

To further his secret plan to gain total rule, he assumed the role of Princeps, or "first citizen" and "one with the people." He deluded the Senate into believing the Republic had returned to its original state. In actuality, all power lay with Augustus. Without the Senate quite realizing what had happened, the Roman Republic had ended and become the Roman Empire, and Augustus Caesar had become its first Emperor.

Augustus's reign of almost 50 years was a period of peace and prosperity. He continued the reforms designed by Julius Caesar to reorganize the government, give jobs to and feed needy citizens, and rebuild Rome. He created a police force to help fight growing crime and a fire brigade to stop the destructive fires that often swept unchecked through the city. He had built or restored more than 80 temples and encouraged growth in road, dock, and harbor building. Word has it that Augustus once boasted, "I found Rome built of sun-dried bricks. I leave her covered in marble."

Augustus Caesar

Compare Julius and Augustus Caesar

Have students make a Venn diagram to compare the achievements and ruling styles of Julius and Augustus Caesar. Begin by drawing on the chalkboard a Venn diagram. Label the parts and start students with one item. Then divide the class into small groups and allow them time to research and complete their diagrams. A completed diagram may look similar to the one below. Have groups share their diagrams with the class.

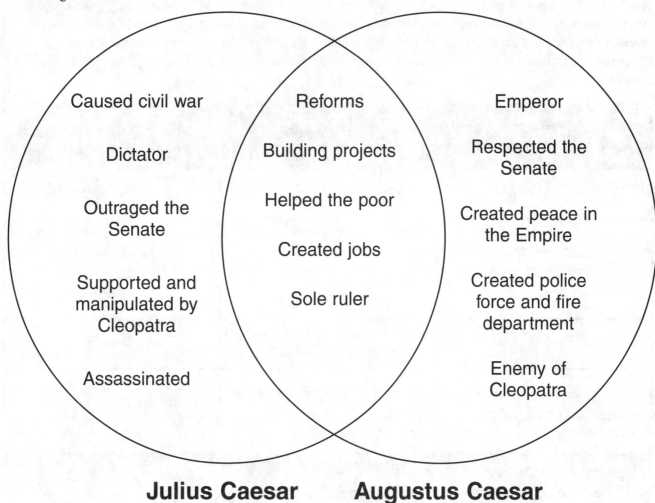

Julius Caesar		Augustus Caesar
Caused civil war	Reforms	Emperor
Dictator	Building projects	Respected the Senate
Outraged the Senate	Helped the poor	Created peace in the Empire
Supported and manipulated by Cleopatra	Created jobs	Created police force and fire department
Assassinated	Sole ruler	Enemy of Cleopatra

Dramatic Dialogue

Imagine Mark Antony and Octavian meeting to discuss ruling the Roman Empire. They decide to divide it in two. This is a very important meeting for both of them, because they each want total control. However, they agreed to compromise.

Have students work in groups of four to write a dialogue for this meeting. Assign each student a role: Octavian, Octavian's inner voice, Mark Antony, and Mark Antony's inner voice. Have students include what each character is thinking as well as what he actually says.

Have each group perform their dialogue for the class. Discuss which dialogue seemed the most authentic, provided the most information, and seemed the most underhanded. Talk about what can happen in everyday situations if what someone says doesn't match what he or she truly thinks.

What's in a Name?

Octavian had many names in his lifetime. Make a chart on the board like the one below. Have students refer to the passage **Octavian/Augustus Caesar** (pages 61–62) to help you list his different names and describe each stage in his life and the reason for his name change.

Have students make a chart for themselves and list the different names that they might go by at home or at school (nicknames, family names, etc.) Why might different people refer to them by a different name? (relatives might use one name, pet names used by parents, nicknames by friends, etc.) What names or titles might they use in the future? (Mr./Mrs., Dr., Sam, Sir, different married name, hyphenated name, etc.) What is the purpose of using different names or titles? (to show affection, respect, etc.)

Name	During what part of his life?	Why?
Gaius Octavius	Birth and early childhood	Legal name
Gaius Julius Caesar Octavianus	When adopted by Julius Caesar	To show he was the son of Julius Caesar
Caesar Octavian	When he inherited power after Caesar died	Shortened name
Princeps	When he was secretly plotting to gain total control	To fool the Senate
Augustus Caesar	When he became Emperor	To show the power and respect he enjoyed

Name	Who calls you this?	Why are you called this?
Colton James	School records	Legal name
Cole	Family and friends	Shortened name
C.J.	Friends on soccer team	Another Cole on team
Pumpkin Head	Parents	Baby nickname

64

Emperors of the Pax Romana and Beyond

Following the death of Julius Caesar, different people tried to gain power in the Republic. Caesar's adopted son, Octavian, defeated the others in 31 B.C., with the help of Mark Antony. Octavian proved a worthy leader who introduced many reforms and rebuilt Rome. In 27 B.C. he was awarded the title "Augustus," or "respected one," by the Senate.

Augustus Caesar's rule marked the beginning of rule by emperors and the Pax Romana, or Roman Peace. The Pax Romana lasted for about 200 years, during which time the Empire was united. To raise money and conduct a population census, Augustus ordered all citizens of the Empire to return to their place of birth to be counted and taxed. The Bible says that "a decree went out from Caesar Augustus that all the world should be taxed." It was this decree that caused Mary and Joseph to leave their home in Nazareth and return to Bethlehem, where their son Jesus was born.

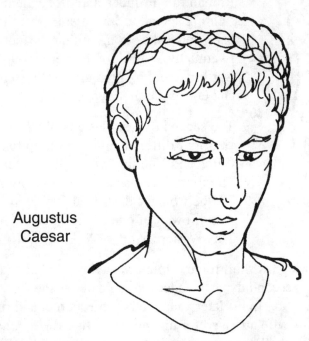

Augustus
Caesar

Towards the end of his life, Augustus worried about who would succeed him. He wanted to avoid the kind of problems that arose after the death of Julius Caesar. Augustus had no son of his own, but he wished to keep the title of Emperor in the family. He decided on his stepson, Tiberius. To ensure a smooth transition, Augustus began to share power with Tiberius and include him in important decision-making.

Augustus Caesar died in A.D. 14, and Tiberius stepped right into position. For the next 200 years emperors followed this process. He chose his successor from his natural family, or he adopted someone into the family to carry on the heritage. Four family lines, or dynasties, ruled the Roman Empire. Some emperors ruled wisely and brought great fortune and peace to the Empire. Others were foolish, vain, or cruel. Each of the dynasties ended in a violent uprising against an unfit or unpopular emperor.

Five members of this first dynasty, known as the Julio-Claudian, ruled during the Pax Romana: Augustus, Tiberius, Caligula, Claudius, and Nero. During this time, Jesus was ordered crucified by Pontius Pilate, the Roman governor of Judea. Although this was a tragic and important event in the history of Christianity, it meant little to the rulers of Judea or Rome at the time. To them, Jesus was only one of many people killed to preserve peace throughout the Empire.

Emperors of the Pax Romana and Beyond *(cont.)*

The Julio-Claudian dynasty ended in disgrace. The last emperor, Nero, came to power when he was 17 and ruled from A.D. 54–68. A vain and poor leader, Nero was unable to earn the respect of the Senate or the military. Many Romans complained that he was more interested in entertaining himself than in governing the Empire. He was famous for giving musical recitals in which he played so badly that some of his guests would feign death just so they could be carried out.

In A.D. 64 a great fire swept through Rome. Nero blamed the fire on the Christians rather his own neglect. Others believed Nero was glad for the fire—and perhaps even caused it himself—because he wanted to build a new capital. These people claimed, "Nero fiddled while Rome burned to the ground."

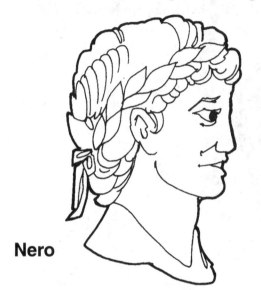

Nero

In A.D. 66 a group of Jews called Zealots rebelled against Roman rule in Judea and drove them out for a time. The fighting spread to Jerusalem, where the Romans fought back under the strong military leadership of Titus. Eventually, opposition to Nero mounted and a bloody civil war broke out. At the age of 32, Nero committed suicide and ended the first dynasty.

The second dynasty lasted only 26 years. During the first year four different emperors tried to control the Empire. Galba and Vitellius were killed. Otho committed suicide. The fourth, Vespasian, reigned from A.D. 69–79. In A.D. 70, the Romans destroyed all of Jerusalem except for the western wall of one of the sacred temples of the Jews. This Western Wall, or Wailing Wall, still stands today.

Titus ruled from A.D. 79–81. During his short reign, Mount Vesuvius erupted and destroyed the cities of Pompeii and Herculaneum. The second dynasty ended as tragically as the first. Its final ruler was Domitian, who ruled from A.D. 81–96. In his later years he became a cruel and ruthless dictator. Finally, fearing for her own life, his wife arranged for his murder. His assassination opened the path for a new line of emperors who would lead Rome into a period of expansion and stability.

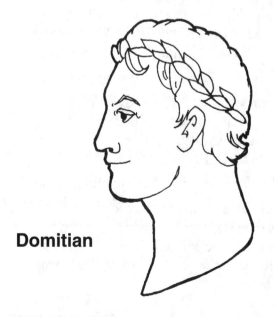

Domitian

The third dynasty was known for its good emperors, beginning with a gentle aristocrat named Nerva. He immediately introduced new policies, such as free speech, to counteract the atrocities of Domitian. Although Nerva only ruled from A.D. 96–98, his reign gave Rome a chance to recuperate from Domitian's harsh domination. Nerva had no son, so he chose to adopt Trajan, a Roman citizen from Spain.

Emperors of the Pax Romana and Beyond *(cont.)*

Trajan was in command of the Rhine army when he became emperor in A.D. 98. He ruled for 19 years, during which time the Empire expanded into Armenia and Mesopotamia. Trajan built new roads and libraries. He improved the life of the citizens by offering low-cost loans to farmers. He provided support for poor children and orphans. Under his leadership Rome entered a period of prosperity and stability.

Trajan's successor, Hadrian, was also born in Spain. Hadrian was a leader with great energy, many interests, and much talent, who ruled from A.D. 117–138. Hadrian was a refined and well-educated gentleman who had a love for Greek culture, art, science, literature, and architecture. He not only tended to matters of state, but also wrote poetry, painted, and designed public buildings. He now had a vast empire to govern and he chose to become as informed and involved as possible.

Hadrian

Hadrian traveled beyond Italy to see firsthand the problems facing his administration. One such problem was another rebellion of the Jews in Judea in A.D. 132. Once again the Romans crushed them. Hadrian was the first emperor to establish fixed borders with massive lines of defense. He is most well known for a wall in Britain that stretched from one side of northern England to the other. He also had constructed in Germany a wall called the Limes, which extended between the Rhine and Danube rivers. During the reign of Hadrian, small settlements around forts and castles became cities and towns.

Hadrian was succeeded by a mediocre emperor who did not involve himself in the workings of the Empire as Hadrian had done. Antoninus Pius reigned from A.D. 138–161. During this time the Empire appeared peaceful, yet there were growing signs of rebellion in many outer regions. Antoninus refused to do anything to contain these outbursts, and they eventually caused his downfall.

His chosen successor, Marcus Aurelius, faced insurmountable problems throughout the Empire. He attempted to protect the borders, but uprisings, rebellions, and invasions increased. Invasions by barbarians from the north became so serious that the headquarters of the Empire shifted from Rome to Carnuntum. He ruled until his death in A.D. 180. The death of Marcus Aurelius marked the end of the Pax Romana, the period in which Rome reached the peak of its cultural and political achievement.

Marcus Aurelius's 19-year-old son, Commodus, succeeded him and was a cruel and unpopular leader who was killed in A.D. 193. Beginning with Commodus, future emperors failed to control the Empire and eventually lost the respect of the Roman army. Further problems with loyalty existed because many of the leaders in central government were now citizens from outer provinces rather than citizens from Rome. By A.D. 200 more than half of the Senate was from outside Rome. Some of these Senators became emperors, as had Spaniards Nerva and Hadrian.

Emperors of the Pax Romana and Beyond *(cont.)*

Septimius Severus began the fourth dynasty of emperors. He came from North Africa and ruled from A.D. 193–211. The Severus dynasty continued after his death, but conditions across the Empire deteriorated. In A.D. 212 Emperor Caracalla granted full citizenship to the entire free population of the Empire in hopes of unifying the vast region, but Rome continued its downward spiral. The last dynasty came to an end with the assassination of Severus Alexander, who was killed by his own soldiers in A.D. 235.

For the next 50 years civil wars shredded the Roman Empire as 25 emperors came and went. The economy was a disaster, invasions by tribes from northern Europe threatened the borders, taxes were at an all-time high, poverty and unemployment were increasing, food was scarce, and different religions caused growing conflict. Throughout the history of Rome the government had fought against Jewish rebellion, and now it also faced a growing number of Christians. Roman leaders felt the Christians were destroying the Empire. In hopes of pleasing the Roman gods, large-scale persecutions of Christians were ordered by the emperors from A.D. 250 through A.D. 311.

One such emperor was Diocletian, who ruled A.D. 284–305. Persecuting the Christians was only one method he used to try to salvage the Empire. Diocletian also introduced major reforms such as setting prices on goods to help the economy, increasing the size of the army to ward off foreign threats, dividing the Empire into four regions to rule it more efficiently, increasing the size of the government, raising taxes, and passing strict laws. Diocletian restored some order, but his reign was harsh and unpopular. He retired in A.D. 305, and his system of control failed. Civil war broke out, and military leaders fought for control of the Roman Empire.

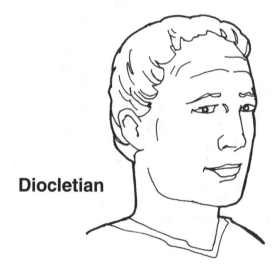

Diocletian

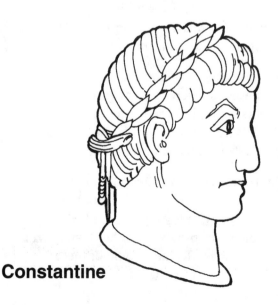

Constantine

One of these military leaders was Constantine, who gained control of and reunited the Empire. He was the first Christian emperor and established Constantinople as its new capital. After the death of Constantine in A.D. 337, his sons and nephews fought for control. By A.D. 400 the Empire was permanently split into two distinct regions. The Eastern Roman Empire and Constantinople would survive another thousand years. The Western Roman Empire, with Rome as its capital, would soon face extinction.

Create Living Statues

Have students research and report on some important Romans.

Preparing for the lesson:

1. Reproduce Emperors of the Pax Romana and Beyond (pages 65–68) for students to read individually or in groups.

2. Reproduce a Speech Organizer (page 71) and a Speech Evaluation Form (page 58) for each student.

3. Make an overhead transparency of the Speech Evaluation Form.

4. Gather picture examples of Roman clothing, headgear, and other props.

5. Bring in a flashlight.

Teaching the lesson:

1. Have students read Emperors of the Pax Romana and Beyond. Discuss the meaning and influence of dynasties. Note the periods of peace and prosperity compared to the periods with harsh or foolish rulers. How much did the prosperity of Rome rely upon its ruler? What other factors contributed to these periods? How is this similar or different than the fate of our country and the president we choose?

2. Randomly assign one of the following famous Romans to each student.

• *Julius Caesar*	• *Titus*
• *Brutus*	• *Trajan*
• *Caligula*	• *Marcus Aurelius*
• *Galba*	• *Caracalla*
• *Vespasian*	• *Constantine*
• *Nerva*	• *Cassius*
• *Antoninus Pius*	• *Tiberius*
• *Septimius Severus*	• *Nero*
• *Diocletian*	• *Otho*
• *Mark Antony*	• *Domitian*
• *Augustus Caesar*	• *Hadrian*
• *Claudius*	• *Commodus*
• *Vitellius*	• *Severus Alexander*

Other famous Romans include Cicero, a famous orator; Pompey, a great military leader; Virgil, Rome's greatest poet; Horace, another famous poet; Livy, a Roman historian; and Ovid, a writer of love poems and legends.

Create Living Statues *(cont.)*

3. Tell students that they are going to research and write short biographical speeches about their Roman figures. The speeches will be written in first person, as if they are the characters describing themselves.

4. Have students also note any clothing or props associated with their character as they research. Tell them they can dress in costume and present their speeches as if they are museum statues come to life.

5. Distribute Speech Organizers to students and have them prepare their speeches. Display the overhead transparency of the Speech Evaluation Form and review the different aspects of the speeches that will be evaluated. Tell the class that "visual aids" include their costumes and props.

6. Assign dates for students to present their speeches as living statues. Since some students will be "frozen" while others speak, schedule only four to six students to speak each day or session.

7. To set up your "museum," have the four to six students who are to speak dress in their costumes and pose as if statues.

8. Assign a student as Lighting Director to handle the flashlight and light each "statue" when it is his or her turn to speak.

9. Turn off some of the lights. Students will be filling out evaluation forms on each speaker during the activity, so you will need enough light to see the Speech Evaluation Forms.

10. Tell students that they have entered a museum where the statues come to life. Have the Lighting Director shine the flashlight on one of the statues, but not in his or her eyes. When the statue is lit, the character gives his or her speech. Characters who are not lit stand as still as statues.

11. Each statue takes a turn speaking and then freezing again. After each session distribute the completed evaluation forms.

12. Once all students have had a turn to be a living statue, compare and contrast the different rulers or other famous Roman characters.

Speech Organizer

Name: _____

Speech date: _____

I. **Introduction**—get audience interested—question, trivia, joke, dramatization

_____

_____

_____

_____

_____

II. **Body**—clear sequence of events, points with supporting details

_____

_____

_____

_____

_____

_____

_____

III. **Conclusion**—summarize and state points, end with strong closing statements

_____

_____

_____

_____

_____

_____

Review your Speech Evaluation Form (page 57) for the criteria of this assignment.

Constantine

Narrators 1–3   **Saul**—father

Venusia—mother   **Cassius**—son

Septima—daughter

Narrator 1: It is May 11, A.D. 330, springtime in the Mediterranean region. The newly built city of Constantinople is finished, and a festival is held for its dedication. There will be games, feasts, and parades for the next 40 days to honor the new capital of the Roman Empire and the emperor who made it all possible. Join Saul and his family as they attend these festivities at the racetrack next to the Great Palace of Constantine.

Saul: How lucky we are to be enjoying such a grand parade. The soldiers are all in their finest uniforms and holding white candles. Here comes the wagon with the golden statue of our great leader Constantine. Bow to the statue to show respect for this fine man who made this all possible.

Venusia: Our children do not realize what is was like for Christian families like ourselves before the rule of Constantine. Before he came into power, great waves of persecution tormented all Christians. The worst was under the leadership of Diocletian around A.D. 300. He ordered mobs to destroy churches, burn books, and break the crosses we use in our worship. Many Christians were fired from their jobs, forced out of the military, attacked, and even killed. It wasn't until Constantine came into power and reunited the Empire that we could worship freely.

Septima: Mother, we have learned a great deal about Constantine and the service he has done for us Christians as well as the Roman Empire. Constantine was the son of a leader in the Roman government. He was with his father on an expedition to Britain when his father died in A.D. 306. The Roman army proclaimed Constantine the new emperor. As he approached Rome in 312 to fight for his leadership, he saw a vision of the cross on the sun. Although he was not a Christian, he believed that this was a sign that his men should fight under the sign of Christ. He had all of his men paint a chi-rho symbol on their shields. His men won the battle, and he became the undisputed Emperor of the Western Roman Empire.

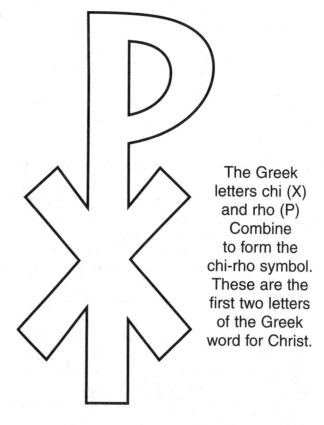

The Greek letters chi (X) and rho (P) Combine to form the chi-rho symbol. These are the first two letters of the Greek word for Christ.

Cassius: In 313 Emperor Constantine used his power to allow all Romans to worship the religion of their choice. This act ended the official persecution of Christians and led Constantine to become an active Christian himself. He contributed vast sums of money to help rebuild churches that had been damaged under previous rulers and to erect new churches. The Roman Senate and many citizens were not happy with his new devotion, and this is one reason why he moved the capital to our new fair city.

Constantine *(cont.)*

Saul: Yes, Constantine was growing more and more displeased with Rome and the Western portion of the Empire. During battles to win leadership of the entire Empire in A.D. 323, he was introduced to this Ancient Greek city, then named Byzantium, which lay between Greece and Asia Minor. He could see that the city offered many natural advantages for a capital. It was accessible by land and by sea, and therefore a great deal of trade passed through the city. At this time many of the richest provinces of Rome lay in the eastern part of the Empire, and his new location would allow easy administration of these areas. Furthermore, Byzantium was located on a narrow peninsula, making it easy to defend from attackers.

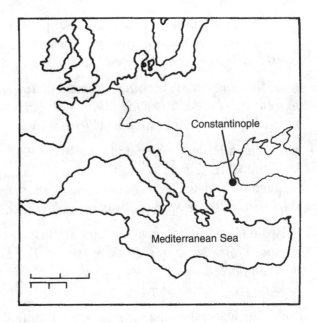

Venusia: Besides, the best soldiers now came from the East. Most western provinces had been weakened by Germanic tribes, and soldiers were losing loyalty. The East also had more Christians than the West. Constantine knew that he would have more support from the Christians, so a move to the East was logical. He decided to rebuild the city of Byzantium and rename it Constantinople after himself. As you can see, our city has become the "new Rome" since it looks much like the original capital in Italy. The Great Palace of Constantine has been built next to this magnificent racetrack. I understand the great leader watches the races from his palace windows!

Saul: After the parade I will take you to the forum, which is paved in marble. In the center stands a huge golden statue of Constantine on a high column. The sidewalks of the main avenue are decorated with hundreds of bronze statues brought in from other Greek cities. Many say they were stolen.

Septima: Oh, Father, can we also visit the public baths? I hear they are built with great walls of marble.

Cassius: I would also like to tour the new church to see the fine mosaics and frescoes.

Saul: Yes, yes, children. But first let's take a moment to honor this great man. Join in as Christian and pagan priests pray for Constantine and the future of our fair city.

Narrator 2: The move from Rome in the West to Constantinople in the East proved to be a wise one. The Western Empire slowly declined into extinction. Influenced by Greeks, Christians, and people of the Orient, the Eastern Empire prospered and led the civilized world for another thousand years.

Narrator 3: During his reign, Constantine became more and more attached to Christianity. His favorable outlook on the church meant many could convert without the fear of persecution or reprisal. On his deathbed in A.D. 337, Constantine was baptized. His nephew, Julian, who became the Emperor in 361, tried but failed to restore paganism. Although less than ten percent of the population were Christians at the beginning of Constantine's rule, by A.D. 400 Christianity had become the official religion of the Roman Empire.

Constantine—Comprehension and Debates

1. How was Constantine able to come into power? (*There were unrest and civil wars throughout the Empire. His father was a high government leader, and when he died, the army elected Constantine as leader. He then had to fight to earn his title as Emperor of the Roman Empire.*)

2. Why did Constantine become sympathetic toward the Christians? (*He saw a vision of a cross as he went into battle. After his soldiers all painted the chi-rho symbol on their shield and won the battle, he felt he had to support Christianity.*)

3. Past Roman leaders persecuted those who did not worship the pagan Roman gods. This included Jews and Christians. Do you think the persecution stopped once the Roman religion was formally changed to Christianity? (*Accept reasonable answers. The fact is, once the religion was changed to Christianity, the Romans began persecuting all those who were not Christians.*)

4. Why did Constantine move the capital to Byzantium in the East? (*The West was in decline because of invasions by Germanic tribes. The East had more Christians and therefore offered more support for his decisions. Byzantium was a good center for trade, well protected, and a good place to administer the rich provinces of the East.*)

5. Under the leadership and support of Constantine, Christianity flourished and became the official and main religion of the Roman Empire. What do you think would have happened to the Christian religion without the support of Constantine? Would it have continued to grow anyway, or would it have died out as other Ancient religions have done? (*Accept reasonable answers.*)

Discuss and Debate: Church vs. State

Lead the class in a discussion of the similarities between the religious persecution in Ancient Rome and that which led our forefathers to come to a new land and establish the United States of America. Remind students that throughout much of history, governments have dictated which religions their people could and should follow. Some governments were tolerant of other religions; others were not.

In Ancient Rome the government dictated the worship of pagan gods and emperors. Leaders in government (state) were sometimes advised by the religious leaders (church), but they were definitely separate. However, as the Christian church became more powerful in the Roman Empire, so did the religious leaders. By the end of the A.D. 300s, church leaders not only gave orders to emperors, but they even punished them. The church had overwhelmingly become a more powerful force than the state.

The Constitution of the United States requires the separation of church and state. Lead a discussion/debate about the pros and cons of a government supporting a particular religion. How has the separation of church and state affected our nation? Why do some people want more religion put back in the government? How do students feel about this?

Legacies of the Ancient Romans

The Ancient Romans were a practical people able to adopt and adapt ideas to suit their needs. Since their main goal was expansion, they mastered the skills necessary for building and governing a vast empire. Part of their lasting legacy to the modern world is embodied by their achievements in many diverse areas.

Designing and Building Great Cities—In places such as Gaul (France) and Britain, there were no organized towns. The Romans encouraged them to build cities in the Roman fashion. Roman towns were made up of networks of streets and blocks. The different blocks contained residential houses, stores, workshops, and bars or saloons. The blocks toward the center of the town were reserved for magnificent public buildings and the open forum, or marketplace, where people could gather to conduct business and discuss local events.

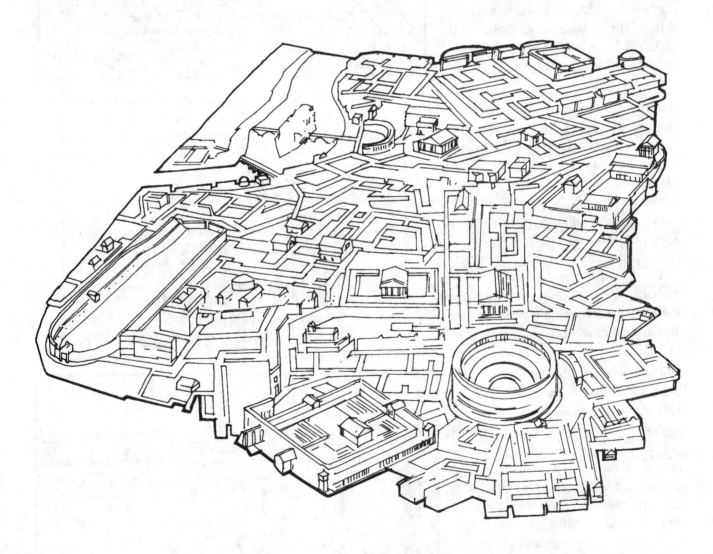

The forum often contained the main temple dedicated to the Roman gods. Around town were other temples dedicated to local gods or other local religions. Public buildings included the bath house and public fountain. Near the open forum was the basilica, or town hall, where meetings could take place. Other structures in a Roman town included theaters, stadiums, and racetracks.

Legacies of the Ancient Romans *(cont.)*

Master Road Builders—To unite their vast empire, the Romans built over 50,000 miles of roads. These roads helped to improve trade and communication throughout the Roman Empire. Many of these roads were paved with layers of stone and concrete. The roads were usually very straight, with a slight hump in the middle so water would drain down the sides into shallow ditches. Roman roads show advanced engineering skills. The Appian Way, constructed in 312 B.C., is still used today by tourists and local residents.

Architecture—Other examples of fine engineering and skillful building are found in the public works of Ancient Rome. Romans perfected the Etruscan arch and combined it with Greek architectural elements such as columns and triangular pediments. These design elements, along with a new building material called concrete, enabled the Romans to create elaborate cities with beautiful temples, coliseums, stadiums, theaters, bridges, and domed buildings.

Plumbing—The Romans were also master plumbers. They designed and built complicated water-supply systems to bring fresh water into their cities. This was done through a series of special channels called aqueducts. Drains and pipelines were constructed to carry rainwater and sewage away from the cities. Most plumbing was made from lead pipes and worked because of gravity. Examples of plumbing systems in bathhouses, public fountains, and household sinks and toilets can still be observed to this day.

Legacies of the Ancient Romans (cont.)

Legal Administration—In order to govern their vast empire, it was important for the Romans to develop and enforce consistent systems of laws and justice. The Romans created professional lawyers, judges, courts, and rules of conduct within the legal system. Laws were first publicized on the Twelve Tables in 450 B.C. Later, as the Roman Empire grew, the laws were codified in a series of written volumes. Roman law helped to civilize the world, because wherever the Romans conquered, they took their legal concepts with them.

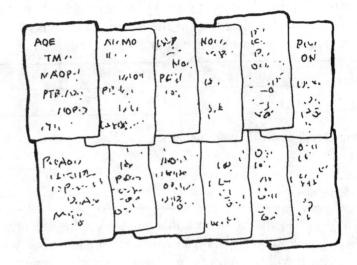

Time and Money—The Romans were great organizers who insisted on accuracy in all things. Our calendars today are based on Julius Caesar's calendar and Latin. Although sundials were invented by the Egyptians and improved by the Greeks, it was the Romans who used them extensively throughout their Empire to record time. It was also the Romans who designed the format of coins with a head on one side and a national symbol on the other.

Entertainment and the Arts—Modern-day racetracks and circuses date to Ancient Rome. In grand stadiums and arenas, gladiators and animals fought in bloody combat, while chariots raced for the glory of their homeland. Roman art is still considered some of the finest in the world. The Roman quest for lifelike sculpture and painting was adapted from the Greeks. Such famous Italian artists as Michelangelo and Leonardo da Vinci used Greco-Roman works as their inspiration. Many Roman works of literature survive today. They are fine examples of creativity and writing skill, and they tell us a great deal about daily life in Ancient Rome.

Our Legacy

A legacy is something received from someone who came before—an ancestor or a predecessor—or from the past. Use **Legacies of the Ancient Romans** (pages 75–77) to think about our cultural achievements. Below, list five things that our culture may leave as a legacy to future generations.

1. _____
2. _____
3. _____
4. _____
5. _____

From your list, choose the one that you believe has the most potential to be a lasting legacy. Use the outline below to help you organize your thoughts. Then write a paragraph about why you think this achievement will be an important legacy. Share your paragraph with the class.

Paragraph Outline

Introduction: _____

_____

_____

Supporting Detail #1 _____

_____

_____

Supporting Detail #2 _____

_____

_____

Supporting Detail #3 _____

_____

_____

Conclusion: _____

_____

_____

Roman Architecture

The Ancient Romans built magnificent structures that included Greek pillars and pediments and Etruscan arches. Have students research several prominent Roman buildings and design a Roman building of their own.

Preparing for the lesson:

1. Gather samples of Roman architecture from books, posters, etc.

2. Gather for each student:

   - 1 piece of 8 ½" x 11" (22 cm x 28 cm) white copy paper
   - 12" x 19" (30 cm x 48 cm) sheet of dark-colored construction paper
   - scissors, glue, ruler, and permanent black marker

3. Make at least one example yourself before teaching the lesson.

Teaching the lesson:

1. Display several examples of different Roman structures (temple, bridge, forum, etc.) Have students note the use of Greek features such as the different styles of pillars and the triangular pediments on the top. Also point out the use of the Etruscan arch in buildings and bridges.

2. Lead students to take note of the horizontal sections (layers) of the structures. Some are thick with large arches and pillars, and some are narrow with designs carved into them.

3. Distribute the materials to the class. Have students think and plan what they wish to make. Have them draw horizontal lines onto their white copy paper and cut apart the sections.

4. To make arched layers, have students fan-fold the horizontal sections and then cut an arch shape into the folded section. (This is like cutting out a line of paper dolls.) Encourage students to use a variety of arch sizes.

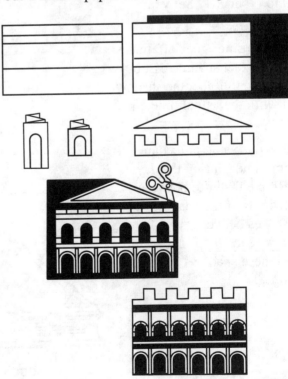

5. Have students create a top for their structure. This could be a triangular pediment or other Roman style feature.

6. Direct students to glue their white sections onto the construction paper. When the glue is dry, have them use a black permanent marker to outline and draw different features, such as bricks, carvings, designs, pillars, pediment murals, etc.

7. Trim the edges of the construction paper to fit. Display the buildings on a bulletin board. Overlap structures to give the illusion of a Roman city.

Make a Simple Sundial

Although the shadow clock was not an original invention of the Romans, it was they who took the sundial to the countries of the Roman Empire. The Roman sundial consists of two parts—a surface onto which a shadow falls and an indicator that causes the shadow. This indicator is known as the gnomon. Make your own simple sundial.

Materials:

- pencil (gnomon)
- ball of modeling clay
- 8 ¹/₂" x 11" (22 cm x 28 cm) sheet of white paper
- box top or bottom at least 8 ¹/₂" x 11" (22 cm x 28 cm)
- tape
- compass
- sunshine
- timer
- clock or watch

Directions:

1. Tape the sheet of white paper to the box top or bottom so the sundial's surface is raised.

2. Place the ball of modeling clay at one short edge of the paper. Push the pencil into the clay ball, making sure it stands as straight as possible.

3. Find a level and sunny spot to place your sundial. Make sure it will not be shaded at any time of the day.

4. Use your compass to locate north/south/east/west. Turn the sundial so that the edge with the gnomon (pencil) faces exactly south.

5. Starting early in the morning, mark the shadow made by the gnomon (pencil). Set your timer for one hour.

6. When the timer goes off, trace over the exact shadow cast by the gnomon. Label the shadow mark with the actual time of day.

7. Follow this same procedure several times during the day. Notice the distance between the lengths of the shadows and the spaces between the shadows each hour. How could these shadows be used to tell time?

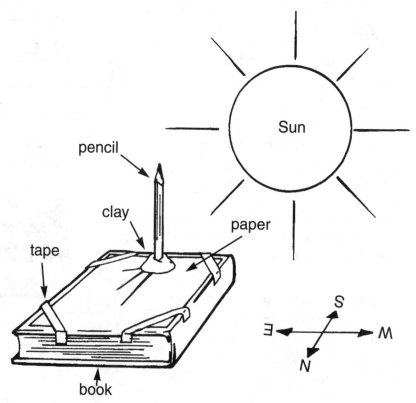

80

Design a Personal Coin

The Ancient Romans made coins from gold, silver, and bronze. Their style of coin design is still used today. Have students create their own coin using the crayon-resist technique.

Preparing for the lesson:

1. Gather for each student two sheets of 18" x 18" (46 cm x 46 cm) white drawing paper.

2. Provide scissors, glue, pencils, metallic crayons (gold, silver, bronze), tempera washes (brown and black), and paintbrushes.

3. Provide a light source (flashlight or overhead projector) for tracing the silhouettes.

4. Gather pictures of Roman coins, and make at least one example yourself before teaching the lesson.

Teaching the lesson:

1. Display the different examples of Roman coins. Have students notice that typically the silhouette of a leader appears on one side and a national symbol on the other. Usually the coin had the name of the leader and a motto, or short expression of a guiding principle.

2. Tell students to pretend they are the new Roman Emperor. They will design and create their own personal coin. Tell them they will work at their seats and take turns tracing their silhouettes.

3. Distribute white drawing paper, pencils, and scissors. Have students draw a large circle free-hand on the paper and cut out both sheets together so that they match. The circles need to be as large as possible, yet need not be perfect—Roman coins certainly weren't. Have students hold their paper circles together and make a mark on the inside tops of both sheets so that they can match them up again later.

4. Have students choose and draw a national symbol on one paper circle. Around the edge of the circle and surrounding the symbol they should write their motto. Brainstorm with the class possible symbols and mottoes.

5. Have students take turns getting their silhouette drawn on the other circle. To draw a student's silhouette, tape or pin his or her paper circle to the wall. Have the student stand in profile in front of the paper. Shine a light source on the student's profile. With a pencil, trace around the silhouette on the paper.

6. Have students use the coin examples to help them add profile details to their silhouette. They may wish to add Roman head gear, jewelry, etc.

7. Once both sides of the coin are drawn, have students choose a metallic crayon to trace over all of their drawing and writing. Tell them to make the crayon thick and heavy so it will resist the tempera paint wash.

8. Have students paint over the crayon on both circles with tempera paint wash. Let the paint dry.

9. Have students match up the two sides of their coin, painted sides out, and glue them together. Punch a hole in the tops and hang the coins from the ceiling with string or yarn.

Latida, a Roman Lady of Leisure

Narrators 1–9

Marcus—father

Garan—younger son

Darius—head slave

Julian and **Flavia**—kitchen slaves

Latida—mother

Servius—older son

Etrusia—daughter

Sarina and **Cassandra**—dressing slaves

Narrator 1: Roman society had a very definite social scale based on wealth and birthright. Your social class determined where you lived, the job you held, the clothes you wore, and the rights or privileges you were entitled to under Roman law. Although the wealthy upper class made up only two percent of the population, they controlled the Empire through the Senate and enjoyed special legal privileges and lesser punishments.

Narrator 2: Members of the upper class included the Emperor, other nobility, Senators, and high-ranking military and government officials. The majority of Romans were in the middle class. This included businessmen, shopkeepers, traders, farmers, and soldiers. Occasionally, members of the middle class became wealthy enough to ascend into the more privileged class. Even the poorest noncitizens and slaves could sometimes earn their freedom or advance their status by gaining wealth. Come now to join Latida and her upper-class family as they introduce you to a life only a few privileged people were able to live in Ancient Rome.

Latida: I am proud to be one of the elite women in Roman society. My husband, Marcus, is a high commander in the Roman army. Most military families are constantly on the move, but we are fortunate that Marcus usually works from Rome and we can have a settled home. Here he makes important decisions regarding where to place soldiers around the Empire for the best protection. He does a fair amount of traveling, but when he is in Rome he conducts most of his business from our home.

Marcus: Our town house, or **domus**, has the same basic design as other upper-class homes in the city. It is all on one level with a front door that opens onto the main hall, or **atrium**. The atrium ceiling is open to the sky. This allows sunlight in. Also, rainwater collects in the small pool in the middle. We store the water for drinking and washing. We also have a small garden toward the back to help give the house an airy feeling and keep it cool during the hot Mediterranean summers. Walking through our home you will notice that the rooms are uncluttered, yet elegant. The walls are brightly painted with murals, and the floors have intricate stone mosaics. The ceilings are high, the doors are wide, and we have very few windows. This is because the streets are noisy and dirty, and thieves abound on every corner. As an added precaution, we have installed on the doors locks that can only be opened with modern keys fashioned from metal.

Latida, a Roman Lady of Leisure *(cont.)*

Latida: We have many rooms in our house. Some are bedrooms and dining areas for the family and friends. We also have a kitchen area where meals are prepared, an office for my husband to conduct business, living and working areas for our many slaves, and a private bath. Other homes of wealthy citizens have shops that open onto the street. As Marcus mentioned earlier, we do not fill our homes with many items. We have only the essential furniture: strong boxes to hold and protect valuables, beds, small tables, wooden cupboards, and couches. Since we do not have many windows, lamps fueled by olive oil are essential for seeing both day and night.

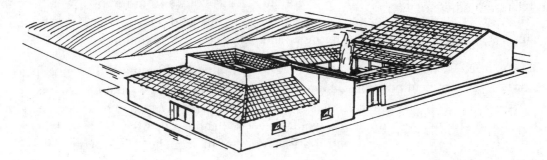

Marcus: We also have a family shrine, or larium, which helps protect our home and family. On the shrine you can see a picture of the **lar**, or protector of family ancestors, offering libations from a drinking horn. We honor our ancestors regularly by visiting their graves and hanging wax masks and portraits of them in our homes.

Narrator 3: By contrast, most common people lived in modest farmhouses in the country or tall crowded city tenements called **insulae**. Most of the tenements were shops and businesses with apartments above them. There was very little space and few luxuries. Many families lived in only one room with no heat or running water. All water was collected from public fountains. Since they had no kitchen, simple meals of bread, beans, lentils, fish, and sometimes a little meat were bought and eaten at roadside "bars." The city insulae also lacked sanitation, so disease was widespread. One-fourth of the babies did not live past their first year, and half of all children died before they were age ten. Fires and crime were other hazards. Although Augustus Caesar had organized the first police force and fire brigade, property and lives were commonly lost in these crowded tenements.

Latida: Marcus entrusts the running of the household to me. I enjoy the responsibility of overseeing our estate, although I do very little of the work myself. I have a number of slaves. Many non-Romans consider the life of the wealthy to be a crowded affair with little privacy. Most upper-class families own 400–4,000 slaves, each with a specific task. Here comes my trusted friend and head servant, Darius. I count on him to help keep things running smoothly day to day, and since we knew you were coming, I have asked him to plan a special dinner party in your honor. Greetings, Darius! Please accompany our guests to the dining room with my husband and seek out our children. I must hurry and dress for the evening.

Latida, a Roman Lady of Leisure *(cont.)*

Marcus: My wife is much too humble. She works very hard around the house making sure things are just right for myself and the children. Not all wealthy women take part in overseeing their homes. Many rely solely on slaves. It is no wonder that so many of them are bored and spend much time gossiping or primping with the latest fashions and make-up. Roman women enjoy many freedoms not experienced in the rest of the world. Women run the household, raise the children, teach their daughters domestic skills, and many help their husbands with the family business. Women can own property, slaves, and their own businesses. Some occupations women can hold include priestess, midwife, hairdresser, and doctor. Naturally, a woman's status comes from her own wealth or that of her husband. Since all property and wealth is controlled by the husband once married, it is not uncommon for a woman to remain single, and therefore independent, once her husband dies.

Darius: This is true, Master. However, women do have limited legal rights and cannot speak before the Senate or hold government positions. I am very proud of my mistress, though. She is very keen and has helped you on many occasions to make difficult decisions. Why, she has even been known to speak publicly at the forum, something you would never see happen in Athens! Here we are at the dining room. Please make yourselves comfortable on one of the couches. I see young Servius and Garan coming, so I will bid you a good evening.

Narrator 4: A Roman dining room was called a **triclinium**. Romans used a low rectangular table with three wide couches around it. Each couch held three people in a reclined position. Although dinner parties were grand affairs with entertainment by clowns, dancers, poetry readings, or music, the group of guests was usually small enough to fit around one table.

Narrator 5: Most Romans ate a small breakfast of bread and water. Lunch was also a small meal of meat, fish, and fruit. Many took a rest in the hot afternoon and went to the public baths. The main meal of the day was dinner, or **cena**, which began around two or three o'clock and lasted for many hours. Bedtime was quite early by modern standards.

Narrator 6: Since there was no way to keep food fresh in the warm climate, meat and fish were smoked, dried, salted or pickled to keep them from rotting. Still, food often went bad. Therefore, clever chefs made strong sauces and presented the food in creative ways to disguise the poor taste. Common foods included olives, asparagus, beans, lentils, grapes, fowl, and fish.

84

Latida, a Roman Lady of Leisure *(cont.)*

Servius: Greetings, dear Father and honored guests. I hope you will find our triclinium comfortable. Father, Garan and I would be pleased to entertain our guests while you finish your tasks.

Marcus: Servius is 15 and a full citizen of Rome. He is furthering his studies in rhetoric so that he can gain a position in the government or perhaps become a lawyer. All of our children went to school at age seven to learn the basics in reading, writing, and mathematics. Some wealthy Romans hire tutors from Greece, but I do not want my children to fill their heads with philosophy and science. Garan will also continue his studies once he is a full citizen, but this is Etrusia's last year of school. My wife will keep her at home now and prepare her for the life of an upper-class wife. My children are fortunate. Most boys are taught by their fathers or work in the family trade. Children are all taught duty, loyalty, and to respect their father and Rome. I will leave you now in Servius's capable hands and will join you at the evening meal.

Servius: I have a great respect for my father. He has always treated me fairly and shown me respect. The father, or **paterfamilias**, has a great deal of power in Roman society and make all of the decisions about the family. He alone can decide life or death for his children. A father decides whether or not a baby shall live. It is quite common for a baby to be abandoned outside the city walls, especially if it is a girl.

Garan: Unfortunately, we were not so lucky. You'll be meeting our sister shortly and see what I mean!

Servius: Hush, Garan. As I was saying, up until his death the father has total control of his family. This means that even after a man's children have grown up and have families of their own, he still has control over them and his grandchildren. Once the paterfamilias dies, this power passes to his eldest son. In our case, this is me, and I will assume responsibility for my younger sister and brother.

Garan: Children are viewed by the law as property. Therefore, a father has the right to sell them into slavery or punish them in any way he sees fit. It is no wonder that children obey their father without question. We are very fortunate indeed to have a father who gives his children such respect and does not rule the house with fear and harsh threats.

Latida, a Roman Lady of Leisure *(cont.)*

Narrator 7: Roman children were raised to look and act like little adults. But they also enjoyed dolls, toy chariots, animals on wheels, marbles, hoops, and piggyback rides. It was common for a wealthy household to have a myriad of pets. Dogs acted as companions and guards. Cats, horses, and birds were kept for entertaining the children.

Etrusia: I hope you are not boring our guests. You boys are just like Father, always so serious. It is unfortunate that the vast majority of men in Rome have little interest in poetry, literature, drama, and music. You all seem to consider the arts unmanly. Our only entertainment is dinner parties or the occasional trip to the theater. We do go to the racetrack to watch chariot races, and going to the arena to watch those barbaric gladiator battles seems to be gaining in popularity.

Garan: Just like a girl to talk such nonsense. The gladiators are a fine example of the power of Rome. Who wants to mess with such drivel as literature and art when you can watch an exciting match between man and beast in the arenas or a fight to the death between two slaves? I must say, I'll be glad when you turn 14 and Mother and Father can begin to arrange your marriage. Then we shall be rid of you and your foolish notions.

Servius: That will be quite enough from both of you. Must I remind you that we have guests? I wonder what is keeping Mother.

Narrator 8: Back in the bedroom, Latida was getting dressed with the help of her two dressing slaves. A lady in Latida's social position had to keep up a certain appearance so that there were no rumors about her. Intrigue was an essential part of Roman society and many loved to spread gossip to enhance their own social positions. Dinner parties were carefully arranged so that conversation was diverted away from controversial topics such as politics, administration of the Empire, and military campaigns. Dining conversation usually revolved around domestic scandals and affairs and was peppered with amusing stories and jokes. The Romans could be very rude and coarse. It wasn't uncommon to poke fun at others' weaknesses, physical appearance, or feeble or failed attempts to climb the social ladder.

Cassandra: Roman women take great care with their appearance. My mistress spends much time at the baths and at her dressing table. She likes to start the day with a facial made from flour and milk. Then she applies make-up, styles her hair, puts on jewelry, and dresses in the latest fashion.

Latida, a Roman Lady of Leisure *(cont.)*

Sarina: Here, Mistress. I have prepared a bowl of water scented with various essences for you to wash your face in. I will prepare your toothbrush and cleaning powders as well, so your breath will be sweet.

Cassandra: Let me help you with your hair. It is long and sleek and twists quite beautifully into a fashionable bun. Tonight we will use your beautiful ivory comb—much nicer than those of wood or bone. Combing your hair for styling also helps rid your scalp of those pesky lice. Do you care to wear a hairpiece? Perhaps a braid placed around your bun?

Latida: Whatever you think will look best. Goodness, anyone looking at my dressing table would wonder at what all of these glass bottles and caskets contain.

Sarina: Here is your chalk powder to make your skin pale and the red ochre for your cheeks and lips. I will help you apply the ash to darken your eyebrows and line your eyes. I notice you are now wearing less jewelry. Your daughter, like most girls, loads herself with armlets, necklaces, earrings, and bracelets.

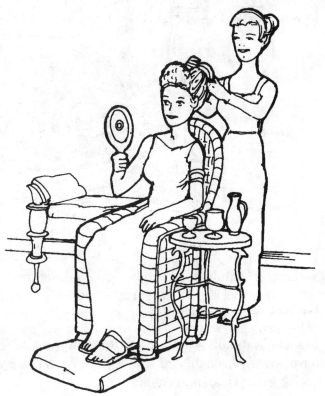

Latida: Etrusia feels she needs to adorn herself with jewelry and make-up since our clothes are quite simple. My underclothes are just a simple shift that doubles as a nightshirt. My main outer garment is the **stola**, or tunic, which falls to my feet. I have many fine stolas of wool and linen in a variety of colors, but my favorites are of cotton from India and silk from China. These Marcus bought for me on his visits to the Eastern Empire. I will gather the stola at my waist and put on a breast band, or **strophium**. I noticed Marcus was wearing his **toga** with the purple banding.

Narrator 9: The usual form of dress for a man was a **toga**, but only citizens of the Empire were allowed to wear one. Slaves and other noncitizens wore only gray tunics or shirts. Middle-class citizens wore plain white togas of wool or linen. However, upper-class males were permitted to wear a purple band that denoted a high office in the government. The bands ran from the shoulder to the bottom of the toga.

Darius: Excuse me, Mistress. If you are finished dressing, the cooks would like to review the menu for the evening meal before serving. The guests are in the triclinium with the children and the Master is working in his office. Shall I go and inform him that cena will be served shortly?

Latida: Thank you, Darius. I shall speak to the cooks and then join the others for dining.

Latida, a Roman Lady of Leisure *(cont.)*

Flavia: Good afternoon, Mistress. The evening's meal has been prepared in several courses and shall be served in your finest dinnerware. I do believe the red Samian pottery will set off the food nicely. We shall begin the meal with eggs, lettuce, olives, snails, oysters, and urchins. The first main dish is Trojan pig. I know this is a favorite of our Master, who loves to carve the pork belly stuffed with sausages.

Julian: It shall be followed by Songbird Surprise, a delicious array of quails and asparagus presented with quail eggs and sauce and a bit more elegant than ostrich or peacock. The final dish is dormouse in honey and poppy seeds. Truly a magnificent menu.

Flavia: Naturally, we have a wide assortment of wines prepared—black, red, white, and yellow. They have already been diluted with water. We assume you wish to use the glass cups. The metal ones leave such a bitter taste in the mouth.

Julian: For dessert we have a fine platter of fresh fruit. Do you wish the musicians to play throughout the meal or only at dessert? We know how the Master enjoys uninterrupted conversation.

Latida: Instruct the musicians to attend the entire meal. Marcus can decide when he wants them to play. I know Etrusia has also prepared a poetry reading. I do believe she would like to have studied in Greece. Ah, well, perhaps we can arrange a fine marriage that will take her to that province. I shall let Darius know that we are ready. Please keep the attendants on their feet so that glasses are kept full and water bowls frequently changed to keep our guests' hands clean. I commend you on your fine work. It is time to offer our guests this wonderful fare and our Roman hospitality.

Vocabulary and Comprehension

Write the following words on the chalkboard for students to copy into their vocabulary books. Remind students to define and illustrate each word.

atrium	**cena**	**triclinium**
paterfamilias	**toga**	**strophium**
domus	**stola**	**lar**
insulae		

Use all or some of the following questions for whole-class discussion, small-group work, or individual assessment. Allow students to refer back to the story while working.

1. Does the passage describe the lifestyle of the majority of Romans in Ancient times? Why or why not? (*No. The upper class represented only 2% of the total population. The majority were middle class or poor.*)

2. What features of Latida's home can also be found in yours? (*Accept reasonable answers.*)

3. How did Latida's home differ from a middle-class home or an insulae? (*It had many rooms, a garden, and an atrium with its own water. Homes of the middle-class and poor had few rooms, and they had to get water from the public fountain. Latida had a kitchen, dining room, and many slaves, whereas most people ate meals at roadside bars.*)

4. Many Greeks considered Roman women to be outspoken and unfeminine. What might have given them this impression? (*Unlike Greek women, Roman women participated in public life— shopping, going to the arena or theater, and attending dinner parties with their families. Roman women were also able to run businesses, own property, and have slaves. Roman women often helped their husbands on business matters.*)

5. Why do you think some wealthy Roman women became bored with their lifestyle? (*Accept reasonable answers.*)

6. The Greeks gave dinner parties called symposiums, in which men ate, drank, and discussed topics such as philosophy, politics, the arts, and sciences. How were these parties different from the Roman dinner parties? How were they the same? (*The Greeks only allowed men to attend the parties. The Romans had both men and women at the party, but they avoided topics about the government or military for fear of gossip reaching others in high positions. The Romans mostly spoke about trivial matters and viewed the party as pure entertainment or a way to show off one's social rank. The Greeks used parties to exchange ideas, learn, and expand viewpoints. Topics at a Greek party were usually controversial and arguments abounded. Both parties had fine food, wine, and entertainment in a special room in the house.*)

A Day in the Life

Research to complete the chart below with information about the social classes in Ancient Rome. After you have completed the chart, use the information to write two diary entries about a typical day of one of the classes. Share your chart and diary with your classmates and discuss the lives of the Ancient Romans.

	Upper Class	Middle Class/ Lower Class	Slave
home			
food			
clothing			
job			
education			
activities			
special rights			

Design a Mail Order Catalog

Have students work with partners to help create a classroom mail order catalog for Ancient Romans living throughout the Empire.

Preparing for the lesson:

1. Gather several samples of mail order catalogs with a wide variety of goods.

2. Write the following categories of goods on the chalkboard:

   - games/toys
   - pottery and vessels
   - grooming items/hair pieces
   - transportation
   - uniforms
   - men's fashions
   - furniture
   - jewelry
   - bathing items
   - weapons
   - women's fashions
   - tools/utensils
   - make-up
   - food/drink
   - religious items

3. Provide writing and drawing materials—pencils, paper, construction paper, crayons, markers, glue, scissors, etc.

4. Decide ahead of time how large each page of the catalog will be and how you plan to bind the pages together—brads, staples, string/yarn, binding machine, etc.

Teaching the lesson:

1. Tell the class to imagine that they are living in Ancient Rome. A wonderful new service has just been implemented that allows everyone from around the Empire to order their goods from a catalog. With the class, brainstorm a name for the catalog. Assign someone to design the cover.

2. Divide the class into partners and have each set of partners choose a category of goods they wish to design and offer in the catalog.

3. Allow students time to study the sample catalogs to see what information is usually included in the description of each item—size, color, feature, price, where it's made, materials it's made from, etc.

4. Distribute the writing and drawing materials. Have each set of partners choose a color of construction paper for their goods section. Tell them to draw/color or cut/paste pictures of the goods and write descriptions about them. Remind them to leave space on the binding edge.

5. Bind the sections together and display the catalog so students in other classes can enjoy it.

Compare Weddings

There are many traditions and customs associated with weddings. Have students compare and contrast Ancient Roman with modern-day wedding customs.

Preparing for the lesson:

1. Reproduce a Compare/Contrast Chart (page 41) for each student.

2. Reproduce Weddings in Ancient Rome (pages 93–94) for each student or group of students.

Teaching the lesson:

1. Tell students that the Ancient Romans had traditions and customs for their weddings just as we do today and that together you will research the similarities and differences between them.

2. Distribute the Compare/Contrast Charts to students. Brainstorm with the class categories for wedding customs, such as marrying age, place for the wedding, engagement customs, wedding symbols and superstitions, wedding clothes, preparing for the ceremony, wedding vows, rituals during the ceremony, rituals after the ceremony, wedding food, party, and gifts.

3. Have students list the categories in the middle column of their charts. Have them label Subject #1 Modern Weddings and Subject #2 Ancient Roman Weddings.

4. Give students the homework assignment of interviewing married couples they know to learn all they can about modern customs related to weddings. Encourage them to talk to people from different cultures.

5. Have students write the information regarding modern weddings in the appropriate column on their Compare/Contrast Chart.

6. Distribute copies of Weddings in Ancient Rome. Read and discuss the information as a class. Then have students write the information about Ancient Roman weddings in the appropriate column on their Compare/Contrast Chart.

7. On the chalkboard or overhead projector, draw a large Venn Diagram like the one below. Have volunteers put the information about weddings on the diagram. Then lead the class in a discussion about how Ancient Roman and modern weddings are alike and different. Elicit the ancient origins of some of our modern customs. What are some things they did in Ancient Rome that we no longer do today?

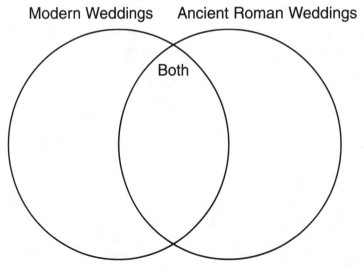

Modern Weddings   Ancient Roman Weddings

Both

Weddings in Ancient Rome

Many customs and traditions surround modern-day weddings. It was no different in Ancient Rome.

Wealthy families arranged marriages for their daughters when they were about 14 years old and considered to be women. Parents considered social status and mutual advantages when they set out to find a prosperous marriage partner for their daughter. Both sets of parents consulted together, and if both families agreed to all the terms, an engagement would take place.

The engagement was celebrated with a special party called a **sponsalia**. During this party the families determined the dowry, or property and wealth a woman would bring to her husband at marriage. The future husband then presented his new bride with gifts. One gift was usually a ring showing clasped hands, which went on the woman's third finger of her left hand. This finger was believed to have a nerve that led straight to the heart. Finally, a contract was signed and sealed with a kiss.

Then it was time to choose a date for the wedding. Days were chosen carefully because some were regarded as unsuitable and unlucky. This was especially true of festival days. Romans thought the best and luckiest time to be married was during the latter part of June.

The simplicity or elaborateness of a wedding depended upon social status and wealth. The most formal weddings, affordable by only the upper class, were called **confarreatios** and were held in the bride's family home.

The traditional dress for a bride in Ancient Rome was a pure white tunic with a bright orange veil. Over this was placed a yellow cloak. The bride's hair was arranged in six braids, and a wreath of fresh flowers was placed around her head. She also wore a special sash woven from wool and tied in a "Hercules Knot." Traditionally, only the bridegroom could untie this knot before the wedding night.

On the day of her wedding, the bride would dedicate all of her childhood toys and dresses to the gods of her father's house. A sacrifice was made, usually a pig or sheep, whose entrails would be read for lucky signs, or omens.

Weddings in Ancient Rome *(cont.)*

The wedding guests would gather at the bride's family home to watch the formal ceremony. The wedding couple sat on separate stools covered with a single sheepskin. Two priests stood in front of the bride and groom to perform the ceremony. Only the bride spoke wedding vows. With these vows she declared that from that day forward she was a part of her husband's family and that her first loyalty was to them.

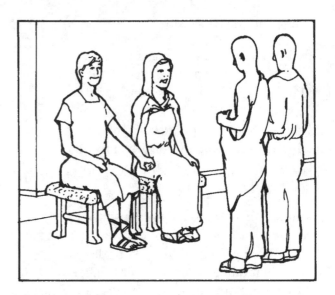

The contract thus sealed, the couple broke a sacred wheat cake and shared it. Then they clasped their hands together as a symbol of their union.

Guests at the wedding then enjoyed a great feast. The wedding cake was distributed just before the end of the celebration.

Once the celebration was over, the wedding guests accompanied the newlyweds from the bride's family house to the groom's. Everyone carried nuts on the journey to throw to the children along the way.

Once they arrived at the groom's house, the bride was carried across the threshold by the guests, for it was considered bad luck to stumble into your new home. The groom then gave his new wife a torch to light a fire in their hearth. The bride tossed the torch into the crowd of guests, who scrambled to get it so they would have good luck.

Make Samian Pottery

In the 1st and 2nd centuries A.D. a glossy red pottery called Samian Ware was very fashionable among the upper class. A wide range of shapes and sizes were created for use in the kitchen, serving, and eating. The pottery was made on a large scale at factories in Italy and Gaul (France) and shipped by the millions all over the Roman Empire and beyond. They became quite popular because they were elegant, easy to clean, and stacked well, allowing for easy storage and transport. Have students make some of this popular Roman pottery.

Preparing for the lesson:

1. Gather enough red clay for each student to have a portion about the size of a softball.

2. Cover all work surfaces with paper or plastic. Provide students with small containers of water and carving tools such as plastic knives.

3. Review the directions for using your kiln if you will be firing the pottery pieces. The pottery does not have to be to be kiln-fired, but firing will strengthen the pottery.

4. Supply clear glossy-coat spray enamel for glazing the pottery.

Teaching the lesson:

1. Remind students that the Romans used a special pottery called Samian Ware at their elaborate dinner parties. Tell them that they will have the opportunity to replicate this pottery using red school clay.

2. Cover the work areas and distribute the materials. Allow students to experiment with pottery designs. Show several examples of jugs, cups, platters, etc., to suggest shapes.

3. Have students carve their names on the bottom of their pottery pieces. Allow several days for the pottery to air dry before firing it in the kiln.

4. Once dry (or fired), spray a glossy coat of clear enamel over the students' pottery. Remember to do this only in a well-ventilated room or outside, without the students present. Spray several coats.

5. Display your students' Samian Ware on a counter with a sign and labels. You may wish to allow students to create construction-paper food to go on their pottery.

The Economy and Trade of Ancient Rome

For all of its major accomplishments, Ancient Rome never developed a complex economy. The Roman economy was mainly concerned with feeding the vast number of citizens and soldiers who lived throughout the Mediterranean region. Therefore, agriculture and trade dominated the economy, supplemented by small-scale industry.

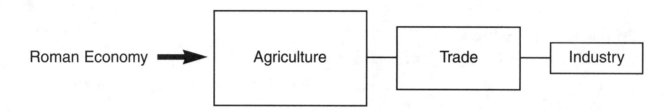

Roman Economy → Agriculture — Trade — Industry

The farmers in Italy grew grains, olives, and grapes. Olive oil and wine were some of Italy's leading exports. However, Roman farming methods were fairly primitive and not very productive. Roman farms produced few crops and required many people to do the work. Farmers were also heavily taxed.

The emperors forced farmers to donate most of their surplus grain to the government as a tax so they could distribute it free to poor citizens. While this made the emperors popular with the masses, it left the farmers with little to sell for a profit. It also left no incentive for farmers to increase productivity, since more product equaled more taxes. As a result, farmers didn't raise enough food for all Rome's citizens, and they had little money to spend and contribute to the local economy.

Roman citizens depended upon the large volume of trade throughout the Roman Empire. Providing enough grain for all its people was a constant challenge that the emperor took very seriously. The leading imports were grains, because they formed the backbone of the Roman diet. Wheat, barley, and corn were needed by civilians and the thousands of soldiers stationed throughout the Empire.

Grains were imported from Egypt, Sicily, Tunisia and other areas around the Mediterranean. Shippers were required to take the grain directly to Ostia, the official port of Rome. Penalties for stopping along the way included deportation or even execution. In Ostia the grain was weighed, checked for quality, and then sent up the river on barges to Rome, where it would be repacked for distribution throughout the Empire.

Although foods dominated the trading industry, there was also a vast exchange of other goods from all parts of Europe, Asia, and Africa. As the young Roman Empire prospered, so grew the demand for luxury items only obtainable from distant lands. Items such as silks from China, cotton and spices from India, ostrich products and ivory from Africa, and mysterious blonde slaves from Germany found their way to Rome via a vast network of trade routes.

96

The Economy and Trade of Ancient Rome *(cont.)*

Trade routes were established on land and sea. The roads built by the Ancient Romans are one of their lasting achievements, and many are still in use today. These ancient highways were not built with trading in mind, however. They were originally built to help swiftly transport huge numbers of soldiers in times of war. They were also intended to carry news from one region of the Empire to another as quickly as possible.

Even the best roads had to contend with bandits and poor weather. Transporting goods by land was slow and expensive. Large loads in wagons and carriages were pulled by lumbering oxen. Horses were faster, but they could only pull light carriages or be ridden. Caravans of camels or donkeys carried loaded baskets called panniers. Some goods were hauled by slaves, who provided cheap labor. Trade by land was only profitable if goods were going short distances or if the cargo was small, expensive luxury items.

Most heavy, bulky, large-volume goods, such as food, wine, oil, and building supplies, were shipped by water. Waterways provided cheap and easy access to all parts of the Mediterranean. Travel was fast if the winds were favorable, but they were also unpredictable and often dangerous. At times the winds stopped, stranding cargo and crew. Ship captains lacked accurate charts and navigational equipment. Therefore, they stayed close to the coastline to navigate, and many vessels were shipwrecked. Archaeologists have found many sunken ships laden with trade goods that offer valuable clues about the lives of people of the Roman Empire.

Rome lived off its imports, and importers were among the wealthiest citizens of the Empire. Many traded goods for goods in a barter system, while others used the silver coins minted by each emperor. In fact, the trade network became so vast that silver Roman coins could be found as far east as India.

Far behind agriculture and trade in importance to Ancient Rome was its industry. The largest was mining. Greece and northern Italy provided marble for the grand building projects commissioned by the emperors. From Spain and Africa came the gold and silver to mint coins and create jewelry, while mines in Britain produced lead and tin for making weapons. Within Italian communities, small-scale manufacturing plants turned out pottery, glassware, weapons, tools, and textiles.

Chart the Economy and Trade of Ancient Rome

Use information from The Economy and Trade of Ancient Rome (pages 96–97) and other resources to complete the following chart.

Agriculture

Food Products

Trade

Imports	Exports

Industry

Mining	Manufacturing

The Roman Empire's Resources

Use the table below to complete the graph and map on pages 100–101.

Product	Country of Origin
wheat and barley	Egypt, Sicily, Tunisia, Italy
corn	Egypt, Russia, Tunisia, Sicily, Sardinia
olive oil	Spain, Tunisia, Libya, Syria, Austria, Greece, Italy
wine	Greece, Austria, Italy
silks	China, Syria
cotton	India
timber	Syria, Yugoslavia, Romania, Lebanon
marble	Northern Italy, Greece
pottery and glass	Italy, France (Gaul)
gold and silver	Africa, Egypt, Spain
lead and tin	Britain
jewels, spices, and perfumes	China, India, Syria, Turkey
wild beasts	Britain, Germany, Africa, Turkey, Algeria

Graph the Empire's Resources

Use The Roman Empire's Resources (page 99) to answer the following questions and complete the bar graph below.

1. Which resource is available in the most locations?

2. Which resource is found in the fewest locations?

3. List the places where food and beverages are found.

4. Which place has the most resources? List the location and the different resources.

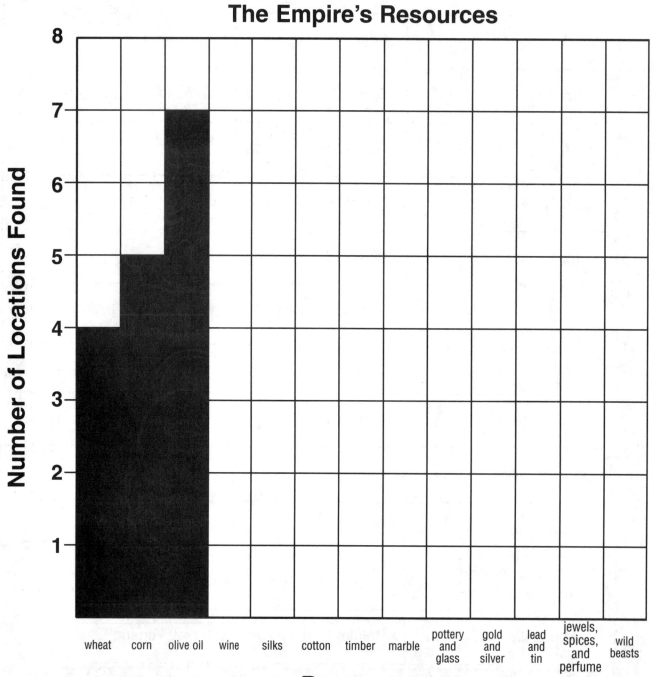

The Empire's Resources

Number of Locations Found

Resources

wheat corn olive oil wine silks cotton timber marble pottery and glass gold and silver lead and tin jewels, spices, and perfume wild beasts

Map the Empire's Resources

Use The Roman Empire's Resources (page 99) to make a resource map of the Roman Empire. Create colored symbols to represent the resources and put them on the map key and the map. Complete the compass rose.

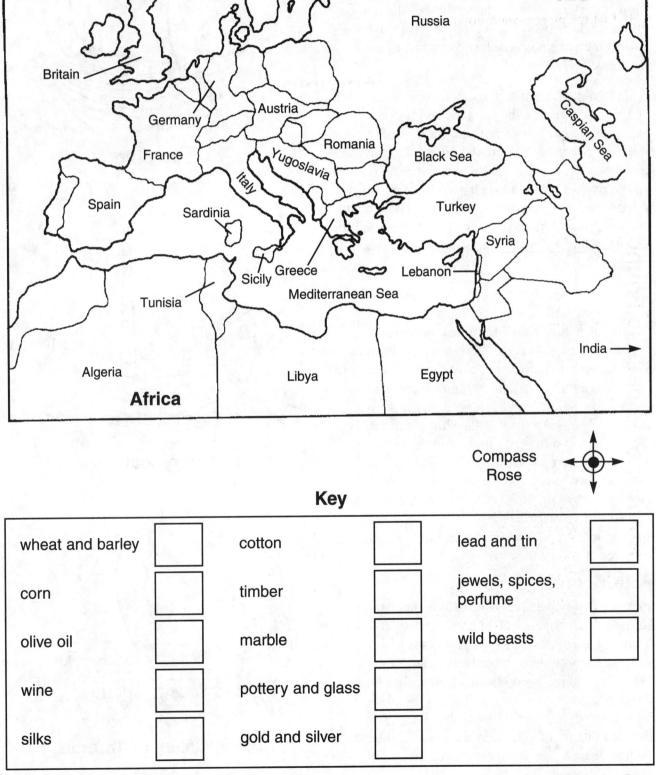

Compass
Rose

Key

wheat and barley		cotton		lead and tin	
corn		timber		jewels, spices, perfume	
olive oil		marble		wild beasts	
wine		pottery and glass			
silks		gold and silver			

A Sea Captain's Log

Imported goods reached Rome by land or by sea. Cargo ships were built with a broad hull able to carry a large variety and volume of goods packed in barrels, wooden boxes, and specially designed storage vessels called **amphorae**. The amphorae were pottery jars whose shape allowed them to be tightly packed together. Although these ships were large, they were not very fast compared to the sleek warships.

Ostia was the port of Rome, about 16 miles inland up the Tiber River. The Romans built large numbers of warehouses in Ostia for the various shipping companies. Here the different goods could be stored and readied for distribution farther up the river. Once in Ostia harbor, the large cargo ships were unloaded onto ferryboats. These boats had a tall mast but no sails. The mast was used for towing. Goods were then moved upriver on small barges.

The harbor was a hubbub of activity. Along with cargo boats, ferries, and river barges there were military warships called **triremes**, or galleys, which were used to keep the waters safe for trade. While merchant ships were built broad and deep to carry maximum cargo, the triremes were shallow and narrow so they could carry many slaves for rowing. The sharp front of the ship sliced through the water, and reinforced towers on the fronts allowed soldiers to board enemy ships. These warships had about 300 galley slaves below deck rowing in rhythm, with little or no rest, and about 300 soldiers above deck ready for action. With such a large crew, the triremes had little room for supplies of food and water.

Activity:

Imagine that you are a sea captain in Ancient Rome. What type of vessel do you command? Write a journal describing your journey. Be as specific as possible in describing weather conditions, activities on board, your feelings, and the purpose for your trip. Tell about the places you go and the things you see or trade. Then draw a detailed picture of your ship and color it. Use the picture as a cover for your captain's log.

Cargo Ship

Ferryboat

Roman Galley or Trireme

Early Beliefs and Worship

When Rome was little more than a small farming community located on the plains of Latium, nature was the people's greatest friend or foe. Farmers rejoiced when the gods favored their farming efforts with enough sun and rain. But they also continually feared that flood, drought, or storm winds would be sent to destroy their crops. They had no doubt that these works of nature were controlled by different spirits or divine powers called **numina**. These primitive people believed that numina were everywhere and that their powers were beyond man's understanding. These people practiced **polytheism**, or the worship of many gods, and their religious beliefs and practices were steeped in **superstition** and ritual.

As Ancient Rome expanded its empire and conquered other people, they began to absorb and accept or modify some of the other cultures' beliefs. The Romans especially adopted and adapted the religious beliefs of the Greeks. Although early Romans thought the numina had no form, they gradually developed the belief that the gods took on human qualities and bodies.

The Romans began to identify their gods with those of the Greeks. Eventually, the two sets of gods could barely be distinguished except for their names. For example, the Greek god Zeus, ruler of the heavens and was king of all the gods, became the Roman god Jupiter. Hera, his wife, became known as Juno. Athena, the Greek goddess of wisdom, war, and handicrafts, became the Roman goddess Minerva.

Zeus–*Greek*
Jupiter–*Roman*

Hera–*Greek*
Juno–*Roman*

Athena–*Greek*
Minerra–*Roman*

Because the people of the Roman Empire came from a wide variety of cultures and heritages, they worshipped in many different ways. The Roman government tolerated this as long as they also paid homage to the official gods of Rome and participated in Roman religious rituals.

Early Beliefs and Worship *(cont.)*

There were two basic ways to worship in Ancient Rome. The first was to worship and make offerings at your own family **shrine**, or lararium. Each morning the family would pay homage to the goddess of the hearth, Vesta, and to other numerous household spirits who were asked to work on behalf of the members of the family. These included Janus, who guarded the home's entrance, and Penates, who looked after the food cupboard.

Family ancestors were also worshipped, and figures called **lares** were kept in the family shrine in their honor. Children were taught from a very early age to pay close attention as their parents offered prayers and petitions to the spirits and gods. Each family believed that it was necessary to offer suitable sacrifices so that the gods would act in the best interests of the family.

The second form of religious practice was a type of public worship conducted regularly at local **temples** or on holy days (holidays) with special festivals. There were many temples, each dedicated to a god the Romans believed was in charge of their daily fate. However, the Romans did not go to the temples to attend religious services. Instead they went to make offerings and sacrifices. Some left coins, pieces of jewelry, small statues of the god, food, and drink. Sometimes messages would be left at the temple asking for something special or for a curse to be placed on an enemy.

Animal sacrifice was common, and incense was burned at the altars where these sacrifices took place. Sacrifices ranged from a single bird to a whole herd of cattle. Different animals were sacrificed in different ways. Larger animals like boars or cows were felled with an axe.

A sacred knife was used to slit the animal's throat open. Its inner organs were examined for **omens**, or signs from the gods. For example, a special priest called a **haruspex** would read the god's will from the shape and condition of the liver. It was a very bad omen if an sacrificed animal's organs were deformed in any way. When the signs had been deciphered by the priests, the organs would be burned on the altar with libations poured from special jugs and bowls. The smoke would ascend to the heavens to appease the gods. Many times the meat from the animal was then cooked and eaten by the faithful in a sacrificial meal.

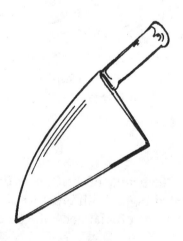

Early Beliefs and Worship *(cont.)*

Other animal-related omens and superstitions included the practice of keeping sacred chickens. The Romans kept a record of how these special chickens ate each day. If they did not eat properly, it was interpreted that the gods must not approve of their plan. Many a battle was determined by the appetite of a chicken! Owls were considered a bad omen. Bees were sacred messengers of the gods and brought good luck. Eagles, the emblem of the Roman legions, were a sign of impending thunderstorms.

Priests conducted the religious rituals, but these men were usually regular citizens who held high positions in public life. Being a priest was only one of their civic duties. The only full-time religious workers were the **Vestal Virgins**, young girls trained to guard the holy flame of the goddess Vesta at her temple in Rome. Of course, as in many ancient cultures, the emperor was considered the chief priest, and temples were dedicated in his honor. During one period of Ancient Roman history, **emperor worship** began when the emperor was declared a god after he died and was required to be worshipped as such.

Still, the attitude of the early Romans toward the gods was mixed. On the one hand they were feared, and many Romans spent a great deal of time and energy trying to win their favor. On the other hand, some Romans were doubtful about the powers of the gods. These people prayed and sacrificed in troubled times, but found the practice dull and unrewarding. Many felt the state religion lacked spiritual fulfillment, so they turned to other religions. Some of the more exotic religions of the East seemed to offer hope of eternal life and more meaning to their daily lives. A number of these cults spread across the Empire along the trade routes. The most popular included the worship of the Egyptian goddess Isis and the Persian goddess Mithras. These involved secret initiation ceremonies, holy secrets, and the promise of rebirth into an afterlife.

The Romans tolerated this diversity of religion as long as it did not interfere with or pose a threat to the Empire. This tolerance did not extend to Jews and Christians. Both of these religions refused to acknowledge and make sacrifices to the Roman gods, and for this they were brutally persecuted. Later Constantine became emperor and decreed freedom of religion. He made Christianity the official religion of the Roman Empire.

Vocabulary and Comprehension

Write the following words on the chalkboard for students to copy into their vocabulary books. Remind students to define and illustrate each word.

polytheism	omen	haruspex
superstition	emperor worship	
shrine	Vestal Virgins	
temples	lares	
animal sacrifice	numina	

Use all or some of the following questions for whole-class discussion, small-group work, or individual assessment. Allow students to refer back to the story while working.

1. How were the Greek and Roman religions similar? (*The Romans adopted the Greek gods and gave them different names.*)

2. What happened to local customs and religion as Rome expanded the Empire into new regions around the Mediterranean? (*People were able to worship as they pleased as long as they also honored the Roman gods and followed Roman rituals.*)

3. What were the two different ways that the Romans practiced their religion? (*They worshipped and gave offerings at family shrines in their homes, and they took part in animal sacrifices and make offerings at public temples dedicated to the state gods.*)

4. Give at least three examples of Roman superstition. (*Keeping sacred chickens and monitoring their eating habits, examining the entrails of sacrificed animals; owls were bad omens; bees were good luck; eagles signaled the coming of a thunderstorm; drought or rain meant the gods were either happy or mad, etc.*)

5. Why did participation in traditional Roman worship decrease? (*People began to doubt the powers of the gods to control their daily lives. Their polytheistic religion offered little spiritual fulfillment, and many found it dull and unrewarding.*)

6. Why do you think Judaism and Christianity became more popular? (*Romans were searching for other religions to fill their spiritual needs.*)

7. Why were the Jews and Christians persecuted and not people of other religions? (*The Jews and Christians refused to worship the Roman gods and emperors along with their own religious practices.*)

Make a Mobile of the Roman Gods

There were many different gods and goddesses in early Roman religion. Each had a particular responsibility in daily life. The Romans believed that most of the gods were related and belonged to one enormous extended family. Work in a small groups and make a mobile displaying the cast of important Roman gods.

Materials:

- construction paper in a variety of colors
- a copy of the cards and pictures (pages 108–112)
- scissors, glue, crayons, markers, or colored pencils
- 15 large paperclips
- hole puncher
- metal hangers or strong wire
- tape
- ruler
- resource materials on the Roman gods

Directions:

1. Cut out the cards and pictures.

2. Color the pictures. In the box on the card write the Greek equivalent of the Roman god. Use resource material to find other information about the gods, such as special symbols, family members, gifts to humans, personality traits, famous myths, etc.

3. Cut pieces of construction paper in half lengthwise. Then cut these strips into squares big enough to glue the cards and pictures onto with a border around the outside.

4. Glue the information card to one side of a construction paper square and the corresponding picture to the other side. The colored border will add excitement to your mobile.

5. Punch a hole in the top and bottom of each construction paper square.

6. Connect the cards/pictures to each other with wire or paperclips and then to a hanger to create a mobile. You may wish to tape the top paperclips to the hangers so they don't shift together when they hang. Bend the top wire to form a clip if you use wire.

7. Display your mobile in the classroom.

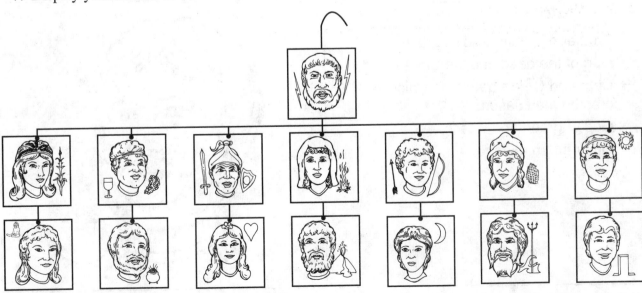

Make a Mobile of the Roman Gods *(cont.)*

Jupiter

- King and father of the gods
- Lord of the heavens
- Controls weather
- Wisest of the gods
- Often in trouble with his wife and sister, Juno
- Children: Apollo, Diana, Mars, Mercury, Minerva, Venus, Vulcan
- Symbols: thunder and lightning; thunderbolts of anger
- Other information:

Juno

- Wife and sister to Jupiter
- Queen of the gods
- Goddess of motherhood and childbearing
- Jealous and angry with husband Jupiter
- Special day: March 1st; Roman women celebrated in her honor
- Other information:

Pluto

- Brother of Jupiter and Neptune
- God of the dead and the Underworld
- Captured Cere's daughter, which created the seasons
- God of greed and wealth.
- Other information:

Make a Mobile of the Roman Gods *(cont.)*

Venus

- Daughter of Jupiter
- Born from sea foam
- Goddess of love and beauty
- Statue honoring her: Venus DiMilo in the Louvre at Paris
- Painting honoring her: "Birth of Venus" by the famous Italian painter Sandro Botticelli
- Other information:

Apollo

- Son of Jupiter and twin of Diana
- God of light and truth
- God of healing, archery, and music
- Associated with inspiration, prophecy, and intelligence
- Handsome, talented, and charming
- Other information:

Vulcan

- Son of Jupiter and Juno
- Thrown from the heavens by his mother; represents home
- Sent Juno a golden chair out of revenge. When she sat down, she couldn't move.
- God of fire and warmth; connected to volcanoes
- God of the forge, weapons, armor
- Other information:

Make a Mobile of the Roman Gods *(cont.)*

Cupid

- Son of Venus
- God of love
- Symbols: carries a bow and arrow to pierce the heart of humans and make them fall in love
- Other information:

Diana

- Daughter of Jupiter and twin sister of Apollo
- Goddess of the moon and hunting
- Guardian of wild animals, especially deer and bears
- Protector of women and of youth
- Legend: if a woman died quickly and without pain, Diana had shot a silver arrow through her heart.
- Despite strong association with women, she despised love as a weakness
- Other information:

Mars

- Son of Jupiter and Juno
- God of war and violence
- Soldiers made sacrifices to him before they went into battle so that they might conquer their enemy.
- Symbols: gleaming helmet with a large plume
- Other information:

Make a Mobile of the Roman Gods *(cont.)*

Vesta

- Sister of Jupiter
- Goddess of the hearth
- Protector of home and family
- One of the first gods to ever have been worshipped
- The Vestal Virgins guard her flame at her temple in Rome
- Other information:

Ceres

- Sister of Jupiter
- Goddess of agriculture and fertility
- Closely associated with farmers, who worshipped her to ensure a good crop.
- Loves springtime and saddened by the coming of winter
- Legend: can only see her daughter in springtime (her daughter was captured by Pluto)
- Festival: Cerelia, celebrated in her honor
- Other information:

Neptune

- Brother of Jupiter
- God of the sea, rivers, streams, lakes, and fountains
- Sea storms a sign of his anger; worshipped by sailors
- Carries a large trident
- Other information:

Make a Mobile of the Roman Gods *(cont.)*

Bacchus

- Son of Jupiter
- God of wine
- Associated with vines and their fruit
- Legend: traveled throughout the world teaching men about the vine and its products
- Jovial trickster
- Theater festivals were held in his honor
- Other information:

Minerva

- Daughter of Jupiter
- Legend: sprang full-grown from Jupiter's head
- Goddess of wisdom, weaving, handicrafts, the arts, and war
- Symbols: carries a spear and wears a helmet and battle robes
- Other information:

Janus

- God of beginnings, departures and returns, doors, gates, and doorways
- Worshipped in every home each morning
- His likeness was put on doors
- Shown with two faces, a young face looking toward the rising sun, and an old face looking toward the setting sun
- Month of January named for him
- Other information:

Match the Planet to the Roman God

Our planets and other celestial bodies were named after Greek and Roman gods. Match the names of seven planets below with the description of the Roman god or goddess. Write the name of the planet on the space before the description. On the lines, tell why you think the planet was named for the god or goddess. What qualities do the planet and the Roman god or goddess have in common?

Jupiter   Mars   Venus   Pluto   Neptune   Saturn   Mercury

_____ 1. He was the father of Jupiter, Neptune, and Pluto. One of the main Roman festivals, the Saturnalia, was held in his honor every winter. During this festival, masters and their slaves would switch roles and exchange gifts.

_____

_____

_____ 2. He was the god of the sea and all other waters. He showed his anger by creating storms at sea and was shown carrying a large trident.

_____

_____

_____ 3. He was the brother of Jupiter and Neptune and lived in the bowels of the Earth. He was known as the god of all the natural riches of Earth and was the god of darkness and death.

_____

_____

_____ 4. He was the son of Jupiter and the god of commerce, trade, and communication. He was the messenger of the gods and wore a helmet and winged sandals. He was also the god of luck and protector of merchants and thieves. He was known to travel far and wide very quickly.

_____

_____

_____ 5. He was considered the lord of the skies and King of the gods. He was married to Juno and had many children. He controlled the heavens and showered humans with foul weather if he was angered.

_____

_____

_____ 6. She was the beautiful goddess of love and beauty who at one time was associated with agriculture and gardening. Legend has her being born from sea foam. Her son, Cupid, shot arrows into humans to make them fall in love.

_____

_____

_____ 7. He was the violent son of Jupiter and Juno. He was the god of war and was worshipped by soldiers before every battle.

_____

_____

Write a Roman Myth

Have students write a mythical story of patriotism or love using the elements from traditional Roman myths. Turn the stories into illustrated picture books and allow students to share them with the class.

Preparing for the lesson:

1. Reproduce a Story Plot Outline (page 118) and an Editing Checklist (page 40) for each student.

2. Reproduce Roman Mythology (pages 116–117) for each student or group of students.

3. Create overhead transparencies of the Story Plot Outline (page 118) and The Writing Process (page 39).

4. Make a two-column chart on the chalkboard to record ideas as you brainstorm with the class problems/conflicts and solutions that students may choose to use in their myths. Head one column Patriotic Myths and the other Tales of Love.

5. Gather drawing materials such as crayons, markers, and colored pencils.

6. Provide each student with a 9" x 12" (23 cm x 30 cm) piece of colored construction paper for the cover of their storybook.

Teaching the lesson:

1. Distribute a copy of Roman Mythology to each student. Read the first portion together as a class and discuss the two main types of Roman mythology (patriotic myths and love tales). Tell students that every story, myth, legend, or tale has some type of problem that must be resolved by the end. Sometimes the story ends well for the characters, but sometimes it does not.

   Under the chart column labeled Patriotic Myths, write the conflict from the Remus and Romulus story. (The brothers fought to see who would be the first founder of Rome.) Discuss how the conflict was resolved and record this on the chart as well (Romulus killed Remus). What are other possible resolutions to this story? (Remus could have won, they could have decided to rule together, they could have both been killed, etc.) Write these possibilities on the chart, too.

2. Divide the students into partners and have them read the Legend of Pyramus and Thisbe. With the class, define and discuss the conflict (Pyramus and Thisbe are in love but forbidden to see each other) and the resolution (they commit suicide). Record on the chart under the column labeled Tales of Love. Elicit from students that this story resembles other famous love stories, such as the story of Romeo and Juliet and that of Queen Cleopatra and Mark Antony.

3. Discuss other ways this problem of forbidden love could have been resolved. (They could have disobeyed their parents and kept trying to get the families together; they could have eloped; the lion might have killed Thisbe, and Pyramus could return to his family, etc.).

Write A Roman Myth *(cont.)*

4. Have students note that Roman mythology is usually very dramatic and emphasizes the glory of Rome and the overwhelming power of love. Have students work in small groups to brainstorm at least two more possible conflicts and resolutions for each type of myth. After the groups have had time to discuss possibilities, come back together to get and record their ideas on the chalkboard chart.

5. Tell students that they will write a Roman myth and may choose either a patriotic or love tale. Students may choose one of the conflicts recorded on the chart or make up one of their own. Remind students to include descriptions of life in Ancient Rome—places, clothing, food, Roman gods, superstitions, rituals, etc.

6. Using the overhead transparencies review The Writing Process and the Story Plot Outline. Distribute a Story Plot Outline to students to use for their prewriting stage.

7. When students have completed their rough drafts, distribute the Editing Checklists and review how students should use the page to revise and enhance their composition.

8. Have students choose 5–10 scenes from their story that they will illustrate for their book. Tell them to write their final drafts so that each scene is on a separate sheet of paper and to leave a wide margin for binding the book.

9. Allow students time to illustrate the scenes they have chosen.

10. Use staples or brads to bind the story pages together within construction paper covers. Tell students to write their myth's title on the cover and also decorate it.

11. Share your class's story books with other classes.

12. As an extension, have students dramatize the legend of Pyramus and Thisbe (pages 116–117), the legend of Cupid and Psyche (pages 119–124), or their own myths.

Roman Mythology

Myths play a crucial role in every society, past and present. These stories, whether recorded or passed down by word of mouth, tell historians what that culture considered important. Myths have a profound influence on the conduct and attitudes of people. Myths are a way in which people use their imaginations to try to understand the world around them. The study of mythology is invaluable to understanding a culture or society.

Roman mythology tells us a great deal about the lives of the Ancient Romans. The religious myths of the Romans were borrowed directly from the Greeks. Roman myths and legends fall into two distinct categories. The patriotic myth deals with the glory of Rome. These stories describe heroic battles and the victory of Rome over less capable enemies. The legend of Remus and Romulus, which describes the founding of Rome, is one example of a patriotic Roman myth designed to glorify Roman past.

Roman tales of love are a tribute to love and family. The gods in the stories don't act as religious beings. Rather, they help or hinder the characters in their struggle against a conflict. The following story is a Roman tale of love.

The Legend of Pyramus and Thisbe

The desert oasis city of Babylon lay far off at the eastern reaches of the Roman Empire. Pyramus and Thisbe grew up together, their families living side by side. They were close childhood playmates, so it wasn't surprising that they fell deeply in love when they became young adults.

Unfortunately, at the same time the youths were discovering their love, their parents had a disagreement. Both families were extremely stubborn and refused to compromise. Because of this feud, both families opposed the courtship of their children. Pyramus and Thisbe were forbidden to see or talk to each other. Instead of the separation killing their love for each other, their imposed break up only made them love each other more.

One day Pyramus found a small gap in the wall that separated the two families' gardens. He called to Thisbe when no one was around, and they agreed to meet there secretly every day. Thisbe lived for that daily time when she could whisper through the wall and catch a glimpse of her love. They tried to be patient, hoping that their families would reconcile, but it soon became obvious that their parents would never change their minds.

Months passed. Finally, Pyramus and Thisbe could no longer bear being apart. They decided to defy their families and elope. This was a painful decision, for both knew they could not stay in Babylon nor see their families ever again. They would be committing treason against their parents. Each day they met at the wall and planned their escape. They arranged to meet at a large mulberry tree on the outskirts of town.

The Legend of Pyramus and Thisbe *(cont.)*

Soon the big day arrived. Thisbe conducted herself as usual so as not to arouse suspicion. As she took the large water pitcher and prepared to go get water, she tearfully bid her mother farewell. Instead of going to the public fountain, she abandoned the pitcher and went to the mulberry tree.

Thisbe waited anxiously behind the tree trunk. Soon she heard footsteps and turned to embrace her darling Pyramus. But it was not he. Instead, she faced a huge mountain lion that had been hurt by hunters. Angry at all humans, it chased Thisbe far out into the thickets. As she ran, her scarf got tangled in a bush and fell from her shoulders. The lion took the scarf in his great jaws and tore at it. Blood from his wounds ran onto the scarf and stained it red. Eventually, the beast grew tired of playing with the cloth and dropped it.

Minutes later Pyramus arrived. He searched all around the mulberry tree but found no one. Then he saw the footprints and tracks in the dust and followed them. In the bushes he discovered the torn and blood-stained scarf of his love. Crying, he carried it back to the mulberry tree. He concluded that Thisbe must have been killed by a lion. Distraught over his loss and calling Thisbe's name, he plunged his sword deeply into his heart to keep it from aching forever. His blood spurted onto the mulberry tree and dyed its pure white mulberries a deep and sinister red.

Meanwhile, Thisbe hid in the thickets until the lion left. She was cautiously making her way back to the tree when she heard her name. Recognizing the voice of Pyramus, she ran back. Breathless and full of hope she reached the tree, only to find Pyramus near death and lying in a pool of blood. Thisbe sat down and gently placed his head in her lap. They declared their undying love for each other and sealed it with a final kiss. Pyramus died in her arms. Heartbroken, Thisbe took up his sword and plunged it into her own heart. She collapsed on the body of her beloved.

The young pair lay dead. Their lifeless bodies were discovered and returned to their distraught parents. The fight that had before seemed so important was forgotten, and the families agreed to live in peace once more. As a declaration of friendship and in honor of their children's love, they agreed to cremate the bodies and bury the ashes in a single urn so that Pyramus and Thisbe could be together forever, as they had wished. From that time forward, the berries of the mulberry tree were red to signify the tragedy that can result from forbidden love.

Story Plot Outline

I. Introduction

A. Character descriptions_____

_____

_____

B. Setting descriptions_____

_____

_____

C. Problems or conflicts to be resolved by the end _____

_____

_____

II. Plot—Sequence of Events

A. Obstacles/scenes leading to the climax

1. _____

_____

2. _____

_____

3. _____

_____

B. Climax—the scene where the problem is solved—peak of excitement_____

_____

_____

III. Conclusion/resolution _____

_____

_____

_____

The Legend of Cupid and Psyche

Narrators 1–12   **Suitors** 1–3

Psyche   **Venus**

Cupid   **Psyche's father**

Psyche's mother   **Apollo**

Zephyr   **Sisters** 1–2

Narrator 1: Long ago a king and queen were blessed with three lovely daughters. The two eldest ones were above average in beauty, but Psyche, the youngest of the three, was the fairest and brightest maiden in all the kingdom. Many suitors came from far and wide to gaze upon the gentle girl, hoping to win her love. Unbeknownst to Psyche, some even deserted the temples of Venus to worship Psyche as a living god instead. This meant trouble.

Psyche: Oh, how I love to walk in our beautiful garden and admire the flowers. I see that many others also enjoy the colorful display, for the garden is always filled with spectators whenever I am about.

Suitor 1: Psyche is so beautiful—and so naive. She believes that we come to see the flowers, but they pale in comparison to the sweet blossom of her face.

Suitor 2: Yes, her beauty is unsurpassed. She truly must be blessed by the gods and created for us to worship, for she is more beautiful than any other living thing. Why else would they have made her so?

Suitor 3: I agree. I understand many are calling her the second Venus, although the girl is completely unaware of it. I imagine Venus is getting quite jealous, for Psyche is more beautiful than the goddess of love herself.

Suitor 1: You shouldn't have said that! Venus might overhear and seek vengeance. We must go quickly!

Narrator 1: Venus did hear. Gazing down at Psyche from Mount Olympus, she called upon her son, Cupid, for help.

Venus: So this is the maiden that everyone is admiring. She is quite beautiful, without a doubt, but am I not a god? How dare they worship a mere mortal and neglect me and my temple. I shall see to it that this nonsense stops at once! When I get through with Psyche, she will wish she had been born as ugly as a toad. Cupid, I have a task of great importance for you.

Cupid: Yes, Mother, whatever you ask of me I will do.

The Legend of Cupid and Psyche *(cont.)*

Venus: Your mother has been gravely insulted. The woman called Psyche plans to undermine my powers. I have a plan to stop her. You must find the ugliest and most loathsome creature on Earth. I will take the creature to Psyche as she sleeps. You can pierce her with one of your arrows, and when she awakens she will be filled with passion for the first creature she sees. The ghastly one will be there to greet her. I will see to it that they marry right away. This should end any ambitions she might have to take my place.

Cupid: Dear Mother, I shall do your bidding tonight.

Narrator 2: Cupid set out to honor his mother's request. But that night when he flew into Psyche's chamber, he too was stunned by her beauty. How could anyone so lovely be trouble? Gathering his courage, he drew his bow and aimed at her shoulder. Suddenly Psyche awoke, and although Cupid was invisible, she gazed directly into his face. Startled, Cupid slipped, and the arrow intended for Psyche instead scratched his own hand. He stood there feeling the sweet poison fill his veins, growing dizzy with joy and love. He knew he could never bring her any harm and quickly returned to Mount Olympus to face his mother.

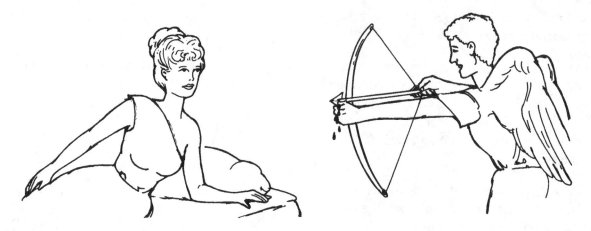

Narrator 3: When Venus heard what happened she fell into a rage and ordered Cupid out of her sight. To punish Psyche she cast an invisible hedge of thorns about her so that no suitor could come near her. The beautiful young princess was very lonely and sad, and her parents could not understand what had happened. Cupid was tormented with grief and refused to do any more work for his mother. People stopped falling in love. There were no marriages and no children were born. Soon the temples of Venus stood empty.

Venus: I see that you must have your way. What is it that you wish?

Cupid: I want the girl. Only with that promise will I turn my attention back to the business of creating love for you.

Venus: So be it, but first you must restore love to the Earth. Then seek out Apollo and explain to him what has transpired. He will know what to do to help you.

Narrator 4: Cupid did as he was asked. Meanwhile, Psyche's parents grew more and more concerned, for as the rest of the world returned to love, their beautiful daughter mysteriously remained alone. Fearing they had angered the gods in some way, they traveled to the Temple of Apollo to make offerings and consult his oracle. They didn't realize Apollo was secretly doing Cupid a favor.

The Legend of Cupid and Psyche *(cont.)*

Apollo: I know you grieve for your daughter. However, Psyche was not meant to marry a mortal. You must take her to the top of the mountain and leave her there. She will become the bride of he who vanquishes both man and god. Go now and prepare her for her fate.

Father: I do not wish to lose my daughter, but we cannot go against the wishes of the gods. I can only imagine the hideous monster that dwells in the mountains waiting to devour my Psyche. This fate has befallen many other princesses who have been sacrificed to appease the gods.

Mother: It is an awful thing we must do, my dear, but I shall get Psyche ready for the journey. Since this is her final day, she shall wear her bridal gown and jewels. The city will shine with torchlight and music will escort her up the steep mountainside. We must attempt to make this a joyous occasion, if only for her sake.

Narrator 5: The day of the wedding seemed more like a funeral. Psyche's family escorted her up the mountain as a flute played a mournful tune. Psyche did not shed a tear and walked in a dreamlike trance. Once at the top of the mountain, she stood waiting, her arms full of flowers.

Father: My dear sweet child. It grieves me to leave you here alone, but Apollo has ordered it. We dare not go against his wishes. We will always remember your gentle, lovely face. I cannot bear to think of your future.

Psyche: Fear not, Father, for I am not afraid. This is what the gods intended, so do not torment yourself with grief. Please dry your tears, for I will be all right. Go now, all of you.

Narrator 6: The wedding party sadly returned to the castle, and at last their cries faded. Psyche stood on the mountain hearing only a great silence. Suddenly the wind began to blow in warm gusts. Her hair came loose and her gown whipped about her like a flag. Then she heard a huge breathy murmur in her ear.

Zephyr: Do not shiver, for I am the West Wind and have come to take you home to a palace luxurious beyond your wildest dreams.

Psyche: I have been expecting a dragon or monster, but your touch is gentle and kind. Are you my intended bridegroom?

Zephyr: I am but your groom's humble messenger. Do not question your fate, for there is much beyond your understanding. Now lean into me and I shall I lift you off of the mountain and carry you like a feather on my gentle breezes. That silver castle on the hilltop is to be your new home. Walk through the courtyard and the great doors will open. A velvet carpet will unroll at your feet. Follow it into the palace. Someday your love will come to you.

The Legend of Cupid and Psyche *(cont.)*

Narrator 7: Psyche did as she was told. Inside the magnificent palace she was led by a floating torch to a fragrant pool to bathe. Invisible attendants helped her dress in sumptuous gowns and jewels. A table was set with the finest golden dishes. Like magic, a banquet appeared and the goblets filled with wine, but still she saw no one. The days passed, and Psyche longed for companionship. Although she had riches beyond belief, she missed her family and friends. One night as she put out the candles in her chamber, she heard a powerful voice speaking very softly in the dark, so softly that the words were like her own thoughts.

Cupid: Do not be afraid, dear Psyche, for I constantly have my eyes upon you. I am your intended husband. The moment I set eyes on you I knew you must be my wife. You are the most beautiful woman in all the world, beautiful enough to make the goddess of love herself grow jealous.

Psyche: Where are you? Why can I not see you? Are you the one who sent for me?

Cupid: Yes, and it was I who built this palace for you, so you must believe in me. Don't try to see me, but know that I will take good care of you.

Narrator 8: Cupid secretly feared that once Psyche recognized him as the son of Venus she would adore him as a god rather than love him as a husband. He decided to test her love before revealing himself to her.

Cupid: Reach out and touch me. Trust in my love for you more than anything else. I must be gone each day, but I will return to your warm embrace every night.

Narrator 8: When the sun rose the next morning, Psyche was alone. But she was so happy she didn't care. Slowly she began to take great pleasure in exploring the castle and the grounds. Day after day she happily returned to the castle to be served by her invisible servants, and night after night she awaited the return of her mysterious but loving husband. As she sat in the dark listening to his soft voice, she wondered how it was that she above all others was allowed this incredible joy.

Cupid: Are you happy, little one? Can I bring you anything?

Psyche: I have so much already, but there are some things that I do wish dearly. You always come at night and I have yet to see your face. The day grows long without you. I wait for nightfall, but some days it seems it will never come. If this is not too much to ask, perchance my sisters could come for a visit? I get so very lonely.

Cupid: You will see me someday, my love, but you must be patient. There are reasons for this, and you must trust my judgment. Bringing your sisters here will only bring trouble. Please do not beg me further.

Psyche: If you say I can't see you, then sadly I must accept it. But please do not keep my sisters from me. It has been many long months since I have seen my family. I hear them weeping for me on the mountain, and I am desperate for them to see how happy I am, so that they can live in peace.

The Legend of Cupid and Psyche (cont.)

Cupid: I cannot bear to see you so distraught. I will have the West Wind bring your sisters to you tomorrow. But be forewarned. This is against my better judgment, and you must be ready for whatever may happen.

Narrator 9: As Cupid promised, the next day the West Wind brought Psyche's sisters to the castle and gently placed them in the courtyard. How relieved they were to find their sister more beautiful and happy than ever! Psyche led them into the castle, where they were attended by the invisible servants. Her sisters saw her great fortune and soon grew jealous. They had married kings for money, but nothing they had could match this luxury. Furthermore, they didn't have the love in their lives that Psyche claimed to have in hers. They questioned Psyche about her husband. Psyche stumbled around the truth, because she knew very little about her true love. Her sisters continued to pry and denounce her husband.

Sister 1: You want us to believe that you are happy, and it appears you want for nothing. But I think this luxury is only a cover for some sinister plot. Where is this wonderful husband we have heard so much about? He must be very vain and proud if he thinks he is too good to meet the family of his wife!

Psyche: Please do not think ill of him, for I know he would be here if he could. You see, if truth be told, I have never actually seen my husband in the light of day. He comes to me only at night. Still, he is the kindest and gentlest creature on Earth.

Sister 2: What? You have never seen this husband you rave about? Mother and Father were right all along. He may not be a man at all, but rather a hideous monster waiting to lure you into his trap. Why else would he hide from you? I'll bet he is feeding you well and laughing as you fall under his spell. Mark my words, the moment you have his child he will be done with you. All of this is only an illusion, my dear, and you must do something about it right now.

Sister 1: She's right. You must not let this monster control you. Take this dagger and use it to put an end to this sham.

Psyche: I won't listen to another word. You are wicked and evil-minded shrews. I never want to see either of you again.

The Legend of Cupid and Psyche *(cont.)*

Narrator 10: With that, the West Wind curled around the two sisters and swept them back to their homes. Psyche was left alone, frightened and longing for her husband. But there were still many hours until nightfall, and her sisters' words stuck in her mind like poisonous thorns. They festered in her head, creating a fever of doubt. As dusk fell, she felt she must see her love to confirm her belief and prove her sisters wrong. She hid a lamp by the bedside. That night, after her husband fell asleep, Psyche lit the lamp and bent over to see his face. There was Cupid, the most loving and beautiful of all the gods. Her heart sang, but as she leaned over to kiss his soft cheek, a drop of hot oil fell from the lamp onto his shoulder and awakened him.

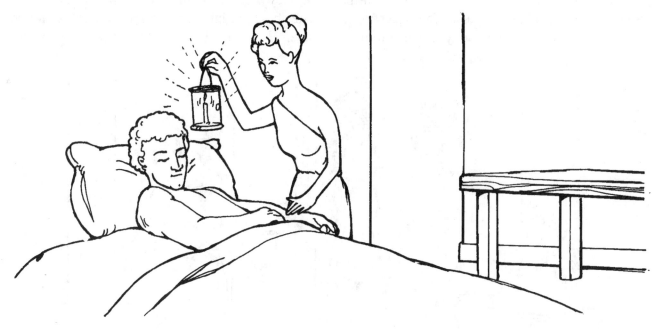

Cupid: Psyche! What have you done? Why have you so wounded me? Have I not been a good husband? Is my word not good enough for you? My heart is torn, for I can never see you again. I love you dearly, but you are not ready to accept my love. Where there is no trust, there is no true love. Farewell forever, dear Psyche.

Psyche: Cupid, no! Please don't leave me! If only I had not listened to my sisters. I am so ashamed. It was my own foolish pride that made me lose my faith in you.

Narrator 11: Grief stricken, Cupid had flown out of the chamber window. Psyche rushed into the courtyard, sobbing and calling his name. As she reached the edge of the garden she heard a sad whistle in the wind. When she looked back, the castle was gone. She stood alone among the weeds and brambles. All of the wonderful things in her life had vanished with Cupid. From then on Psyche roamed the Earth searching for her lost love.

Narrator 12: What became of this love-torn couple? Some say Venus turned Psyche into an owl who sees best at night. Others claim that Venus assigned Psyche some impossible and menial tasks to perform. Magically, she completed each task and won the forgiveness of Venus and Cupid. So Psyche was taken to Mount Olympus to be with her husband and help him with his love labors. On Mount Olympus, Psyche gave birth to Bliss. Many believe it is Psyche's special mission to teach those who wrongly say that seeing is believing. To these people of little faith, Psyche, invisible, whispers in their ears: "None but love knows the secret of love, for the truth is that believing is seeing."

The Jews and the Christians

Augustus Caesar became Rome's first emperor in 27 B.C. During his reign many important events took place to help create an era of peace and prosperity. Travel throughout the Empire was made safe so that trade flourished, and many new goods made their way into Rome. People could now choose from a variety of places to settle and still be protected by the strong Roman military. Many people of all different races were now bound together under one rule. The language, customs, and religions of these various people were accepted by the Roman government as long as they didn't conflict with Roman law.

One of the most important events in the history of the world occurred around 4 B.C. Jesus Christ of Nazareth was born in the town of Bethlehem in an outlying part of the Roman Empire called Judea. The people of this region were called Jews, and their religion was **Judaism**. Jesus was a Jew, and the people who later became his followers were also Jews. Christianity began as a Jewish sect and has its roots in Judaism.

Although the Romans tolerated most religions of the people they conquered, Judaism clashed with Roman religion and law in too many ways. The Jews believed in one true god and refused to recognize any other. This meant they were unwilling to worship the Roman gods or the emperor as a god. The Jews also followed the teachings of their prophets and the strict laws set forth by their god in the **Torah**, their holy book. One of their laws forbade them to make sacrifices, which again conflicted with Roman practice. For these and other reasons, Romans fought the Jews because they believed their religion were a serious threat to the Roman Empire.

Although Judaism was a problem for Roman authorities, it was recognized as a legal religion. As Jesus grew older and began teaching, he attracted a small band of followers, or disciples. This group came to believe that Jesus Christ was the messiah (savior) and the son of God. They called themselves **Christians**. Even though Jews and Christians shared the same basic beliefs, the Jews did not recognize Jesus as the son of God. They believed that the messiah was still to come, and when he did, he would overthrow the Roman government and reunite the Jews. However Christians believed Jesus Christ came to give them the gift of everlasting life.

The Jews and the Christians *(cont.)*

Since the number of people involved in the early Christian sect was quite small, few people throughout the Roman Empire were aware of it. This is why there are few written accounts of early Christianity. Stories of Jesus' life and teachings were collected and recorded between A.D. 100–200 in a part of the Christian Bible called the New Testament. Since these stories are written from the perspective of Christians to teach and inspire other Christians, the stories do not reflect the viewpoints of Jews or Romans.

As Christianity grew and spread, it became a real threat to Jewish as well as Roman authorities. The early Christians concentrated on trying to **convert** other Jews and were met with great resistance from Jewish leaders. Although they were charged with not obeying Jewish law, the Christians insisted that their belief in Jesus and his love were more important than the laws set forth in the Torah. Consequently, **persecution** of Christians came first from the Jews and later from the Romans.

One such persecutor was a Roman citizen and Jew named Saul. He believed that the Christian sect should be wiped out because it did not obey Jewish law. Saul was sure that Jesus was not the messiah, and he tried to destroy the faith. He was heavily involved in arresting Christians and bringing them before Jewish authorities. To further his agenda, he got a letter from the Jewish High Priest authorizing him to travel to Damascus and arrest Christians there. It was his plan to bring these Christians back to Jerusalem to stand trial.

However, according to the New Testament, Act 9, Verses 3–6, Saul was among the many who "saw the light" and converted to Christianity.

> "Now as he journeyed he approached Damascus, and suddenly a light from heaven flashed about him. And he fell to the ground and heard a voice saying to him, 'Saul, Saul, why do you persecute me?' And he said, 'Who are you, Lord?' And he said, 'I am Jesus, whom you are persecuting; but rise and enter the city, and you will be told what you are to do.'"

Saul had been blinded by the light and could not see for three days, but he did not doubt who had spoken to him. It was not until a follower of Jesus Christ touched him that he regained his sight. When he reached Damascus he took the name Paul. From then on, Paul devoted himself to spreading the faith of Christianity across the Roman Empire.

The Jews and the Christians *(cont.)*

Paul was soon accepted into the local Christian community and began preaching in the Jewish synagogue. The Jews were amazed, for here was the man who had come to arrest the Christians now telling them that Jesus was the messiah! Paul continued to convince many Jews to convert to Christianity, even though he was creating great turmoil. Soon he had to be smuggled out of Damascus to avoid being killed by Jewish authorities. When he made his way back to Jerusalem, he tried to join a group of Christian leaders called the apostles, but they were apprehensive about Paul. With the help of other Christians, Paul was finally accepted as one of the apostles.

A new stage of Christianity began. Before, only Jews could convert to Christianity. But now some believed that the religion could be adopted by Jews and non-Jews, or **Gentiles**. Together with the other apostles, Paul began to preach that anyone could be admitted to the Christian faith. He set forth on four great missionary journeys to bring Christianity to the far reaches of the Empire. His first journey took him to Cyprus and Asia Minor. He organized churches and taught Christians to lead them. Paul met with groups of Christians to help them grow stronger. He spoke with Jews and Gentiles about the love of Jesus and encouraged them to convert to Christianity. His inspirational letters to the people he influenced and wished to support were recorded in the Bible in the book of Corinthians.

Paul's three other journeys took him through Syria, Asia Minor, Greece and Macedonia. He traveled over one thousand miles each time and faced great hardships. Eventually, Emperor Nero had Paul arrested and killed. Paul described the difficulties of his missionary journeys in Second Corinthians, Act 11, Verses 23–27:

> "I have worked much harder, I have been in prison more times, I have been whipped much more, and I have been near death more often. Five times I was given the thirty-nine lashes by the Jews; three times I was whipped by the Romans; and once I was stoned. I have been in three shipwrecks, and once I spent twenty-four hours in the water. In my travels I have been in danger from floods and from robbers, in danger from fellow-Jews and from Gentiles; there have been dangers in the cities, dangers in the wilds, dangers on the high seas, and dangers from false friends. There has been work and toil; often I have gone without sleep; I have been hungry and thirsty; I have often been without enough food, shelter, or clothing."

The Jews and the Christians *(cont.)*

As Christianity spread, it became evident to the Romans, too, that something must be done. Christian settlements sprang up around Roman communities, and the Christians were unpopular because they refused to act like other Romans. The Christians kept to themselves and worshipped behind closed doors. Many Romans felt the Christians thought they were superior—like a secret elite club.

Some of the Christian ideas were shocking to the Romans. Roman order relied upon wealth and property as a status symbol, but the Christians denounced money and earthly pleasures. The Romans considered their religion and government to be linked as one, while the Christians saw them as separate. The Christians did not attend public festivals or take part in the activities of their communities because to do so would go against the laws of their religion.

Many Romans feared that the failure of the Christians to honor Roman gods would hurt the Empire. Although the Jews also refused to honor the gods, Judaism was a well-established religion and therefore excused. Soon the Christians' lack of Roman patriotism made them the scapegoat for every natural disaster that plagued the Empire.

In A.D. 64, during the reign of Nero, a great fire swept through Rome for six days and destroyed much of the city. Nero blamed the Christians for the fire. But Nero was a very unpopular leader. Some even believed he started the fire just so he could blame the Christians and turn the people's anger away from himself and onto the unpopular religious group. Nero ordered the Christians to be killed in cruel and barbaric ways, thus beginning a wave of persecution that lasted many decades. Tacitus, a great Roman historian, described what happened:

"First, Nero had self-acknowledged Christians arrested. Then, on their information, large numbers of others were condemned—not so much for starting fires as for their anti-social behavior. Their deaths were made a mockery. Dressed in wild animal skins, they were torn to pieces by wild dogs, or nailed to crosses and crucified, or made into torches to be ignited after dark. Despite their guilt as Christians, and the ruthless punishment it deserved, the victims were pitied. For it was felt that they were being sacrificed to one man's brutality rather than to the national interest."

128

The Jews and the Christians *(cont.)*

By A.D. 100, to be a Christian was a crime punishable by death under Roman law. However, this policy was seldom enforced, because local officials in the provinces actually decided the fate of the Christians under their jurisdiction. Many of these officials were unsure what to do, so they let most Christians alone as long as they didn't make trouble. Still, some Christians were treated cruelly under this law. Many were forced to go into a large arena, or colosseum, to fight lions as entertainment for the Romans.

Many Christians chose to die rather than give up their religious beliefs. These people were known as **martyrs** and became important symbols for the Christian church. Their courage inspired other Christians and even created new converts. Christians buried their dead in **catacombs**, a series of dark underground tunnels and chambers outside the city walls of Rome. The dead were wrapped in linen and sealed into tombs carved in the walls. The tombs of martyrs became shrines decorated with paintings. Although some people believed the Christians hid in the catacombs to avoid persecution, historians say the catacombs were not a secret and, therefore, were used primarily for burials and religious services.

Christians adopted the fish as a Christian symbol. The letters that make up the word fish (in Greek) are the initial letters of the words Jesus Christ—Son of God—Saviour.

Emperor Constantine provided the turning point for the Christians. He believed the Roman government should be tolerant of all religions. He forbade the persecution of Christians and allowed them to worship openly without fear. Churches were rebuilt and congregations grew. Constantine helped Christianity spread throughout the Roman Empire. By A.D. 325 the Christian Church and the Roman State were one and the same. Constantine was officially baptized as a Christian shortly before his death.

The Christian church continued to grow more powerful throughout the A.D. 300s. Church leaders began giving orders to emperors and punishing them for going against their wishes. Just as the Romans had persecuted those unwilling to obey their religious customs, some fanatical Christians were now persecuting **pagans**, or those people who were not Christians or Jews. In A.D. 391 pagan religions were outlawed. Now it was the Christians forcing their beliefs upon others. Intolerance and persecution of those who held different beliefs had come full circle.

Vocabulary and Comprehension

Write the following words on the chalkboard for students to copy into their vocabulary books. Remind students to define and illustrate each word.

Judaism	**Torah**
Christians	**convert**
persecution	**Gentiles**
martyrs	**catacombs**
pagans	

Use all or some of the following questions for whole-class discussion, small-group work, or individual assessment. Allow students to refer back to the story while working.

1. Why wouldn't the Romans tolerate Judaism? (*Jews worshipped only one god and refused to worship the Roman gods or emperors. Jewish law forbade them from making sacrifices.*)

2. How did the Jews and Christians differ in their beliefs? (*The Jews believed a messiah was still coming to free them from Roman control. The Christians believed Jesus was the true son of God and the messiah, who offered them eternal life.*)

3. What historical source do we use to learn about early Christianity? Because it was written solely by Christians, how might this affect the reporting of facts? (*The New Testament in the Bible. It only has the perspective of the Christians and does not tell the story from the point of view of the Jews or the Romans. The stories are biased.*)

4. How did Saul/Paul play an important role in the spread of Christianity? (*He was a Jew and a Roman citizen before converting to Christianity. He was able to travel freely and speak to the Jews to try to persuade them to convert. In spite of enduring many hardships, he went on four different missions to spread the new religion and begin churches.*)

5. Why were the Romans suspicious of the Christians? (*They did not act like the Romans and kept to themselves. They did not participate in sacrifices or other festivals. They did not covet wealth or status. They did not worship in public.*)

6. Why do you think martyrs inspired others to convert to Christianity? (*Accept reasonable answers.*)

7. Why do you think the Christians buried their dead in the catacombs rather than using the public cemeteries? (*Accept reasonable answers.*)

8. When Christianity became the official religion of the Roman Empire did religious persecution stop? Explain. (*No. When Christians became the majority, they began persecuting the minorities—those who were not Christians or Jews—just as they had been persecuted earlier.*)

Compare the Religions of Ancient Rome

Read the numbered statements below that list some of the religious practices in the Ancient Roman Empire. Each statement is true for one or more of the three main religions of that era. Study each statement and relate it to each of the three religions. Then place the number of the statement in the appropriate section of the Venn diagram.

For example, consider this statement: * Welcomed all people into the religion. This statement is true of the Roman polytheism, which encouraged all people to worship their many gods, and of Christianity, which attempted to convert people to believe in their one god. It is not true for Judaism, which only allowed Jews. Therefore, the * has been placed on the Venn diagram in the section where the Christianity circle overlaps the Roman polytheism circle. It is not inside the Judaism circle.

Religious Statement

1. Believed in one god.
2. Believed in many gods.
3. Believed that Jesus was the messiah.
4. Did not believe that Jesus was the messiah.
5. Accepted some of the beliefs of other religions.
6. Religion played an important role in daily life.
7. Carried out sacrifices at public temples.
8. Worshipped in churches.
9. Worshipped in temples and homes.
10. Persecuted the Christians.
11. Persecuted the Jews.
12. Persecuted the pagans.

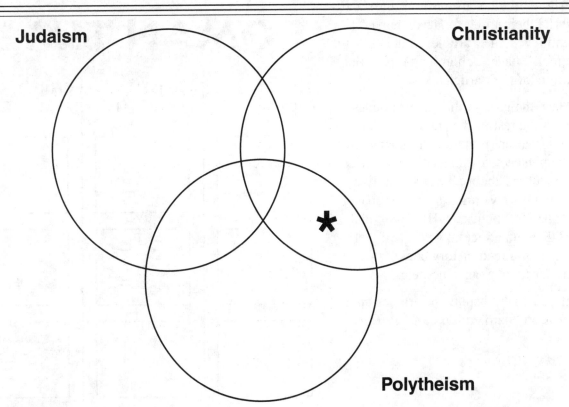

Judaism **Christianity**

Polytheism

Headline News

Newspapers in Ancient Rome were made by professional copyists who spent long hours writing out pages by hand. The pages were sold to the general public. These newspapers contained much of the same information of newspapers today—reports of trials, notices of births and deaths, announcements of public shows, news items, and some advertisements. Have students write articles from the different perspectives of an Ancient Roman, a Jewish, or a Christian reporter. Then discuss how facts might be reported differently depending on the writer's perspective.

Preparing for the lesson:

1. Gather writing materials for each group of students.

2. Write these or other headlines on the chalkboard: Fire Destroys Rome—Christians Blamed; Christian Catacombs Revealed; Martyrs to Fight Beasts in Arena; Constantine Vows Freedom of Religion; Saul or Paul? The Great Conversion; Christians Denounce Paganism.

3. Provide resource materials regarding Ancient Roman religions. Allow students to use Early Beliefs and Worship (pages 103–105) and The Jews and the Christians (pages 125–129).

Teaching the lesson:

1. Tell the class that they are going to be Ancient Roman newspaper reporters for the *Roman Times*. They will work in groups to write articles and editorials for the paper regarding some major religious events.

2. Divide the class into six groups. Assign each group a headline describing a major religious event. Distribute writing materials to the groups and tell them that they will write three articles to go with their headline. Each article will be about the same event, but each will be told from a different perspective: Roman, Jewish, and Christian.

3. Allow time for groups to discuss and write their articles. Have them edit and revise their articles in their group. Finally, have each group prepare final drafts of their articles.

4. Have the groups share their articles with the rest of the class. How did the information in the articles change as the perspective changed? What does this tell us about all news reporting? Can any news program or newspaper be totally unbiased? How will this realization affect how you will feel when you read history books, newspapers, magazines, etc.?

5. If you wish, display the articles on a bulletin board entitled *Roman Times*.

ROMAN TIMES

ROMAN PERSPECTIVE	JEWISH PERSPECTIVE	CHRISTIAN PERSPECTIVE

Map Paul's Missionary Journeys

Paul made four missionary journeys to spread Christianity. His final trip took him back to Rome for his trial and execution. Use the map on page 134 to trace Paul's travels. The cities that he visited are listed in chronological order. Use reference and add those from the journeys to the map. Use a different color to trace the path of each journey. When you have finished, complete the key at the bottom of the map labeling each box with the correct journey. Answer the questions at the bottom of this page.

Journey 1	Journey 2	Journey 3	Journey 4
1. Antioch (Syria)	1. Antioch (Syria)	1. Antioch (Syria)	1. Caesarea
2. Salamis	2. Tarsus	2. Tarsus	2. Sidon
3. Paphos	3. Derbe	3. Iconium	3. Myra
4. Attalia	4. Iconium	4. Antioch (Asia Minor)	4. Lasea
5. Antioch (Asia Minor)	5. Antioch (Asia Minor)	5. Ephesus	5. Malta
6. Derbe	6. Troas	6. Beroea	6. Syracuse
7. Antioch (Syria)	7. Philippi	7. Corinth	7. Rhegium
	8. Thessalonica	8. Beroea	8. Puteoli
	9. Beroea	9. Philippi	9. Rome
	10. Athens	10. Troas	
	11. Corinth	11. Ephesus	
	12. Ephesus	12. Cos	
	13. Cos	13. Rhodes	
	14. Caesarea	14. Tyre	
	15. Jerusalem	15. Caesarea	
	16. Tyre	16. Jerusalem	
	17. Antioch (Syria)	17. Caesarea	

Questions

1. Which journey(s) took Paul to Asia Minor? _____

   to Greece?_____ to

   Italy?_____

2. Which journey covered the most miles? (Use a ruler to find the answer.) _____

   _____

3. Where do you think Paul's home base was for his missionary operations, and why do you think

   that? _____

   _____

Map Paul's Missionary Journeys *(cont.)*

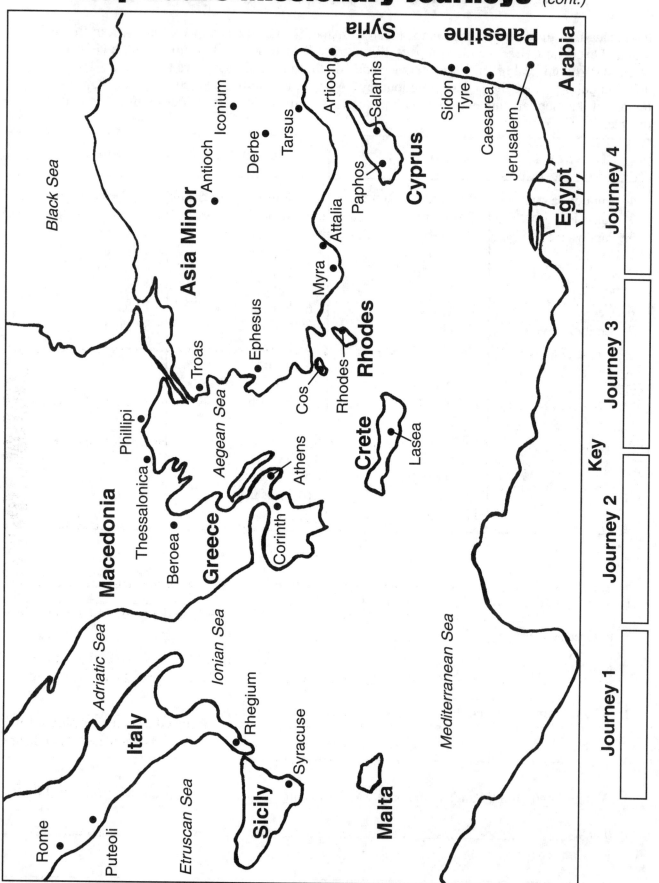

Write a Descriptive Poem

Have students use figurative language to write a poem about a journey into the catacombs.

Preparing for the lesson:

1. Reproduce a writing web (page 136) and Editing Checklist (page 40) for each student.

2. Make an overhead transparency of The Writing Process (page 39).

3. Gather writing materials, dictionaries, and thesauri.

Teaching the lesson:

1. Distribute the writing web sheets to students. Read aloud the description of the catacombs. As students silently read along with you, have them imagine that they are Christians in Ancient Rome and what it would be like to take a journey down into the catacombs.

2. Tell students that they are going to write poems describing their journey into the catacombs. Their poems should answer the questions on the web. Encourage students to use a variety of figurative language such as metaphors, similes, personification, alliteration, and rhyme. Review examples and the definition of each type of figurative language.

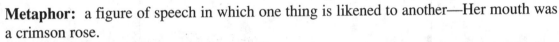

Metaphor: a figure of speech in which one thing is likened to another—Her mouth was a crimson rose.

Simile: a figure of speech in which unlike things are compared with the words "like" or "as"—He was strong as an ox.

Personification: a figure of speech in which a thing or idea is given the qualities of a person—Their eyes danced with merriment.

Alliteration: a repetition of the initial sound of two or more words—Bees buzzed from blossom to blossom.

3. Use the overhead transparency to review The Writing Process. Tell students to use the web with their prewriting.

4. Have students think of words and phrases that apply to each question on the web. Encourage them to consult dictionaries and thesauri to find descriptive words, and remind them to use a variety of figurative language.

5. Distribute writing materials and tell students to write at least one detailed sentence or phrase for each part of the web. Have students read aloud their ideas to help the class get ideas. Then have students organize their sentences and phrases into a rough draft.

6. Distribute the Editing Checklists. Review with students how to use them to enhance their rough drafts. Then have students write their final drafts.

7. Allow time for students to share their poems with the class. Display the poems on a bulletin board or combine them to form a class book of poetry.

Write a Descriptive Poem *(cont.)*

The catacombs were underground tunnels built by the early Christians. The long, dark corridors had tombs carved into the walls. This is where Christians buried thousands of their dead. The entrances were located outside of the city walls, because it was against Roman law to bury the dead in the city. Bodies were wrapped in sheets of linen and sealed in the tombs. Christian symbols and paintings adorned the walls, especially near the tombs of martyrs. Religious and funerary ceremonies and services were held in the catacombs. Christians carried oil lamps to light their way through the damp passageways.

Imagine that you are a Christian in Ancient Rome. Use the web below to organize your thoughts. Then write a descriptive poem about your journey into the catacombs and share it with your classmates.

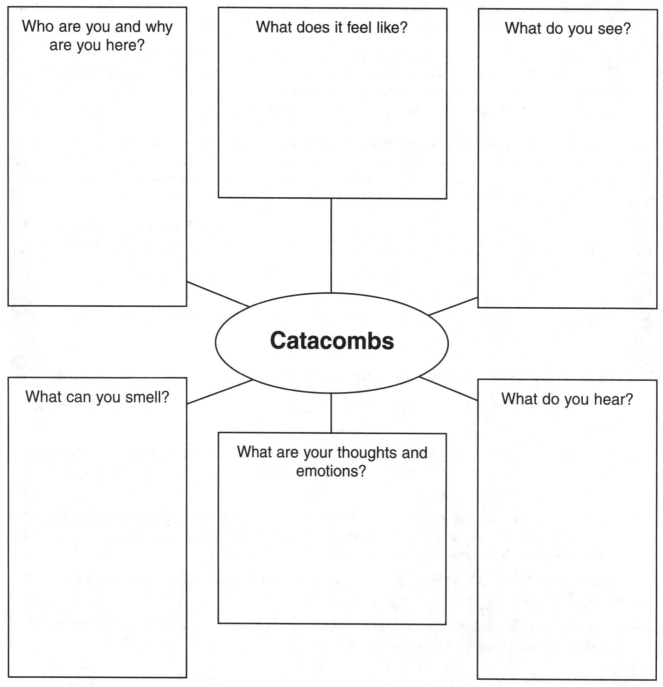

Who are you and why are you here?

What does it feel like?

What do you see?

Catacombs

What can you smell?

What are your thoughts and emotions?

What do you hear?

Servius the Student

Narrators 1–5   Servius—student
Garan—younger brother   Etrusia—younger sister
Timone and Xenatis—friends

Narrator 1: One of the many responsibilities of the head of the family, or paterfamilias, was to make sure that his children were educated and became good Roman citizens. Children were taught to be worthy of the traditions of Rome and to be honest, virtuous, and dutiful toward their father and the Empire. There were two choices for education in Rome—home or school. Join Servius and his classmates as they take you on a tour of the Roman educational system.

Servius: Welcome, my friends. We begin our tour at the local primary school, or **ludus**, where wealthy boys and some wealthy girls are taught from ages seven through twelve. Of course, our education truly begins at home. We learn obedience from our parents. We learn about the gods and how to keep them happy. From an early age boys and girls take part in religious ceremonies. My younger brother and sister are still students here at the primary school.

Garan: To say I don't like it here is an understatement! Every day I am escorted to school by a slave who makes sure I am prepared for the day's lessons. Many mornings I am barely awake. Classes begin at dawn, and lessons last until midday. Our teachers are very strict and require complete attention and obedience. It is not uncommon for a student to be beaten for any sort of misbehavior or wrongdoing. One time a boy contradicted the teacher and was flogged with a leather whip.

Etrusia: Although Garan paints a bleak picture, the teacher disciplines us so that we learn to be respectful. We speak only if we are asked a question, and we always complete our assignments. We have learned to read and write in Greek and **Latin** and to do simple mathematical calculations on the abacus.

Narrator 2: Dozens of different languages were spoken throughout the Roman Empire. In the west Latin and in the east Greek were the standard languages used. The Romans introduced writing to northern Europe. They used the Latin alphabet, which has 22 letters. Roman numerals are still used today, although not for mathematics. But they are used in outlines, for labeling book volumes, and on clocks and watches.

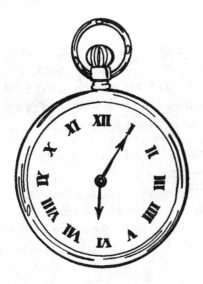

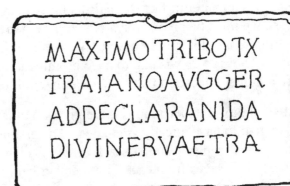

Servius the Student *(cont.)*

Etrusia: Although I am fortunate to have been given the opportunity to come to school, I must say I will not miss the rigorous, repetitious, and mostly boring lessons. This is my last year at school. Mother must now prepare me to master the more important domestic skills if I am to marry a wealthy Roman. I wish Father would have let us have a Greek tutor, or **pedagogue**, like Timone has.

Timone: When I was six my father entrusted me to one of our Greek slaves. As you know, slaves are treated in a variety of ways in Rome. Some work very hard and live like animals. Others, like my trusted friend Sophles, are treated like one of the family. Sophles was a teacher in Greece and is highly knowledgeable in reading, writing, mathematics, the arts, literature, philosophy, and the sciences. Sophles is responsible for my appearance and for teaching me how I should behave in different situations. His care and instruction prepared me to enter the **grammaticus**, or secondary school. Many other wealthy Roman families have Greek tutors for their children.

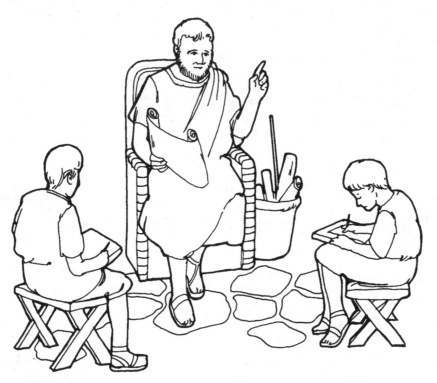

Servius: As a matter of fact, Xenatis and his pedagogue are waiting for us at the grammaticus as we speak, so we must be on our way. Not all boys are able to move on to secondary school. Most children in the Empire are illiterate or have only a basic education because they are needed in the family trade or business. Those of us wishing to have prominent positions within the government or to practice law require a higher education that only wealthy families can afford. Ah, here we are. Greetings, Xenatis.

Xenatis: Hello. I understand you are giving a tour of my alma mater. Although I am glad to help you, I'm also glad to have already graduated. The grammaticus was much more strenuous than I had imagined. We read scroll after scroll of famous Greek and Latin literature and memorized long, complicated passages from each. I remember being questioned constantly by our teachers not only about the content, but also about the grammar and figures of speech used by the authors. And the writing assignments! I dulled more than my share of styluses, and I'm still picking beeswax from under my fingernails!

Servius the Student *(cont.)*

Narrator 3: Students in the grammaticus wrote their daily assignments on special wooden tablets covered in melted beeswax. When notes were no longer needed, the wax was often smoothed and reused. Occasionally, wax tablets were bound together to form a book, but it was more customary for important texts to be written in ink on papyrus scrolls.

Narrator 4: These scrolls were more permanent than the wax tablets, but also more expensive. Paper was made by pounding together the fibers of the papyrus reed, then pressing, and polishing the sheets until they were smooth. Papyrus was used for important documents, especially those with a legal purpose. The very best books were written on a substance called **vellum**, made from the skin of a kid or lamb. Vellum was very durable. The sheets were thin enough to create a beautiful writing surface. But vellum was very expensive and required many hours to prepare.

Narrator 5: The ink used by the Romans was made from soot mixed with resin, wine dregs, and cuttle fish secretions. A tool called a **stylus** was used for writing. They had a point at one end that was used to transfer ink onto papyrus or vellum and to scratch text into wax tablets. The other end was a flat surface used to smooth out, or erase, unwanted text on the wax. Ink pots were fashionable with the Romans. They came in a variety of shapes and sizes. Many of the upper-class displayed their wealth by having beautiful inkpots inlaid with patterns of gold and silver.

Servius: We read and write a lot here at the grammaticus. Here's the school library. We glued the sheets of papyrus or vellum together to form a scroll, or a long strip attached to two dowels. We read them by unrolling them from one dowel and rolling them up with the other. The scrolls are stored in drumlike containers. Our "books" have to be copied by hand—a slow and painstaking process mostly performed by Greek slaves.

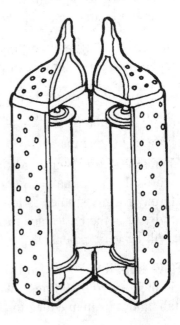

Servius the Student *(cont.)*

Timone: Xenatis and I depended upon our pedagogues to support us at home with our studies, and we learned many more subjects, including advanced calculations in mathematics, weights and measures, and the art of **rhetoric**, or effective and persuasive speaking. Do you wish you had a pedagogue, Servius?

Servius: Primary school trained me well to be disciplined in my studies. Garan may dread his studies here, but he'll enjoy the athletics. We participate in a variety of physical activities such as running, jumping, wrestling, and swimming. There is a terrible toughening-up process.

Xenatis: I certainly wouldn't want to go through that again! We had to swim the river rapids and avoid the rocks. We had to endure many hardships without complaint. How we survived and graduated with honors is mystery only the gods can unravel.

Servius: My father has said very little about my progress, but I believe he is proud of me. Lately I have been accompanying him when he gives important speeches at the forum, and he let me attend a dinner party last week at the home of an important patrician. When I am home and he is conducting business, he allows me to be there with his clients. He says it is good preparation for becoming a respected citizen and paterfamilias. And it's good practice to reinforce the teachings of my rhetor.

Timone: That's right, you are working with a professional public speaker now to further your studies. This will prepare you for a number of professions, such as law, the military, and politics.

Xenatis: Working with a rhetor is far more enjoyable than grammaticus. It is fun to write a speech in which you present and argue various points of view. I have read a few of your essays, Servius, and you show promise.

Servius: Thank you, dear friend. My rhetor requires that I write many different types of essays. But it is not only words that help make a good speech. Tone, diction, and gestures are also important. Father has agreed to pay for my studies as long as I continue to work hard. Eventually I would like to go to Athens to study. It is the best place to study rhetoric, and some of the most famous teachers live there. However, it will be very expensive.

Timone: Have faith in the gods and your fate, Servius. You are a good student. Now let's get back to the ludus and pick up your siblings. We can stop at a food stall on the way home for a midday snack. All of this talk about Roman education has made me hungry!

Vocabulary and Comprehension

Write the following words on the chalkboard for students to copy into their vocabulary books. Remind students to define and illustrate each word.

ludus	**grammaticus**	**stylus**	**Vellum**
rhetoric	**Latin**	**pedagogue**	

Use all or some of the following questions for whole-class discussion, small-group work, or individual assessment. Allow students to refer back to the story while working.

1. What determined the type of education you received if you were a child in Ancient Rome? (*Your class—if you were wealthy you could hire a tutor or go to school. If you were poor you worked with your father to learn a trade or were hired out for work. Your sex—if you were a boy you could go on to further education. Wealthy girls were often taught to read and write, but then they had to learn domestic skills and how to run the household. Your father—the Roman father made all decisions. It was up to him how much education you would receive and where you would be educated.*)

2. In what ways did Roman teachers discipline students? Do you think this type of discipline might work in schools today? Why or why not? (*They taught students to be respectful, to speak only when asked a question, and to make sure all their work was completed. Accept reasonable answers for the other parts.*)

3. Would you have preferred to be taught by a Greek pedagogue or attend the local ludus? Why? (*Accept reasonable answers.*)

4. What subjects or activities taught in Ancient Rome are no longer taught in school today? (*Latin and Greek, Roman numerals and the abacus, memorization of literature passages, writing on wax tablets, and the "toughening-up" process of athletics.*)

5. You have participated in rhetoric lessons. List the different speeches or presentations you have made in your school career to date. Did you practice gestures and the tone of your speech? Did you attempt to persuade anyone with your speeches? If so, you were practicing the fine art of rhetoric.

Compare Educational Systems

Use the information from Servius the Student (pages 137–140) and other resource material to complete the chart below. Be sure to make your entries as detailed as possible so you can use them to write an essay, give a speech, or participate in a debate comparing Ancient Roman to modern education.

Roman Education		Modern Education
	School Levels/ Students' Ages	
	Subjects Studied	
	School Supplies	
	Discipline/ Rules	
	Higher Education	
	Home Schooling	
	Education for Girls	

Compare Educational Systems *(cont.)*

Lead students in other activities that further their understanding of the Ancient Roman educational system as compared to their own. Allow them to use information from this unit and other research material to prepare.

School Days—Use the directions on pages 37–41 and the chart on page 142 to have students write a comparison essay describing the similarities and differences between education in Ancient Rome and today. Have students write their final drafts on pages they tape together end to end. Use dowels or paper-towel tubes to form the ends of a scroll.

Education Timeline—Make a class time line showing the education of a wealthy Ancient Roman boy from birth to age 18. Then have students make an education time line of their own showing their education/age up to present day and their planned further education. Discuss with students how the time lines are similar and different. Ask students what they will need to do to reach their educational goals

Educated at home by parents about Religion and Empire duties	Enter ludus (primary school) to learn basic reading, writing, and math May be tutored by Greek pedagogue instead	Some enter grammaticus (secondary school) for further studies	Private education by a rhetor
1 2 3 4 5 6	7 8 9 10 11	12 13 14	15 16 17 18

Is It Rhetorical?—Rhetoric is the art of speech making. Servius and his classmates studied rhetoric in order to pursue careers in politics and law. Have students practice their rhetoric by preparing and delivering to the class a persuasive speech for or against Roman educational techniques. Have students focus on one aspect of Roman education for their speech, such as the benefits of having a Greek pedagogue or an argument against the severe punishment of students in classrooms. Refer to the directions on page 56 and the chart on page 142. Review the Persuasive Speech Organizer (page 57) and the Speech Evaluation Form (page 58) with students. Remind them that in addition to their words, eye contact, vocal tone, and gestures can help influence or persuade their audience as well as their words.

The Big Debate—Divide the class into two debate teams. One team will prepare a defense for Ancient Roman education while the other team prepares one for modern education. Follow the directions for leading a debate on page 45. When the debate is over, discuss the strong points of each system. Have we incorporated any Roman techniques into our modern day educational system?

Learn Some Latin

Latin forms the basis of many languages such as French, Spanish, Italian, and English. Latin also shows up in English prefixes, root words, and suffixes. Understanding Latin can often help you understand the meaning of a word. Reproduce pages 144–147 to make a Latin matching game for your class or for each student. Cut apart the boxes and have students practice matching the Latin words with the related words in other languages. Be sure to keep the original as an answer key.

Latin: **familia**	Latin: **mater**	Latin: **pater**
French: la famille Spanish: la familia Italian: la famiglia English: family (familiar)	French: la mere Spanish: la madre Italian: la madre English: mother (maternity)	French: le pere Spanish: el padre Italian: il padre English: father (paternity)
Latin: **soror**	Latin: **frater**	Latin: **niger**
French: la soeur Spanish: la hermana Italian: la sorella English: sister (sorority)	French: le frere Spanish: el hermano Italian: il fratello English: brother (fraternity)	French: noir Spanish: negro Italian: negro English: black

144

Learn Some Latin *(cont.)*

Latin: **terra**	Latin: **mare**	Latin: **coelus**
French: la terre Spanish: la tierra Italian: la terre English: earth (terrain)	French: la mer Spanish: el mar Italian: il mare English: sea (maritime)	French: le ciel Spanish: el cielo Italian: il cielo English: sky (celestial)
Latin: **status**	Latin: **clarus**	Latin: **dies**
French: l'etat Spanish: el estado Italian: la stato English: state	French: clair Spanish: claro Italian: cliaro English: clear	French: le jour Spanish: el dia Italian: il giorno English: day
Latin: **annus**	Latin: **hodie**	Latin: **hieri**
French: l'an Spanish: el año Italian: il anno English: year (annual)	French: aujourd'hui Spanish: hoy Italian: oggi English: today	French: hier Spanish: ayer Italian: ieri English: yesterday

Learn Some Latin *(cont.)*

Latin: **amare**	Latin: **legere**	Latin: **dicere**
French: aimer Spanish: amar Italian: amare English: to love (amiable)	French: lire Spanish: leer Italian: leggere English: to read (legible)	French: dire Spanish: decir Italian: dire English: to say (diction)
Latin: **studere**	Latin: **unus**	Latin: **duo**
French: etudier Spanish: estudiar Italian: studiare English: to study	French: un Spanish: uno Italian: uno English: one	French: deux Spanish: dos Italian: due English: two (dynamic duo)
Latin: **tres**	Latin: **quattuor**	Latin: **quinque**
French: trois Spanish: tres Italian: tre English: three	French: quatre Spanish: cuatro Italian: quattro English: four (quadrilateral)	French: cinq Spanish: cinco Italian: cinque English: five (quintuplets)

Learn Some Latin *(cont.)*

Latin: ## sex	Latin: ## septem	Latin: ## octo
French: six Spanish: seis Italian: sei English: six	French: sept Spanish: siete Italian: sete English: seven	French: huit Spanish: ocho Italian: otto English: eight (octopus)
Latin: ## novem	Latin: ## decem	Latin: ## homo
French: neuf Spanish: nueve Italian: nove English: nine (November)	French: dix Spanish: diez Italian: dieci English: ten (December or decimal)	French: l'homme Spanish: el hombre Italian: il omo English: man (homicide)
Latin: ## viginti	Latin: ## centum	Latin: ## mille
French: vingt Spanish: veinte Italian: venti English: twenty	French: cent Spanish: ciento Italian: cento English: hundred (century)	French: mille Spanish: mil Italian: mille English: thousand (millimeter)

Roman Numerals

The number system developed by the Ancient Romans is still used today for many things. Our Arabic number system differs in many ways from the Roman system. Study the information below; then use this page to complete the activities on page 149.

Arabic Number System

Uses ten symbols:

0   1   2   3   4   5   6   7   8   9

This system is also called the decimal system. We use a decimal point and place value to indicate what a symbol means. The value of a symbol depends on its place in a number. For example, the symbol 5 changes its value depending on its place value, or relation to the decimal point.

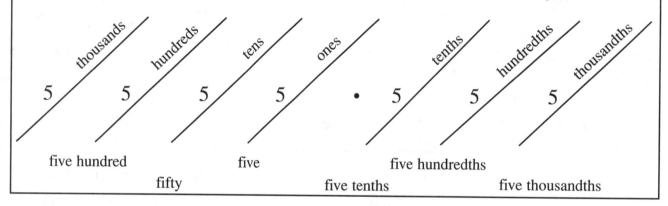

five hundred   five   five hundredths

fifty   five tenths   five thousandths

Roman Numeral System

Uses seven symbols:

I   V   X   L   C   D   M

I = 1   V = 5   X = 10   L = 50   C = 100   D = 500   M = 1000

The Roman numeral system uses these seven symbols and adds or subtracts their values to indicate the number.

I = 1
II = 1+1 = 2
III = 1+1+1 = 3
IV = 5-1 (because the I comes before the V) = 4
V = 5
VI = 5+1 = 6
VII = 5+1+1 = 7
VIII = 5+1+1+1 = 8
IX=10-1 (because the I comes before the X) = 9
X = 10
XI = 10+1 = 11
XII = 10+1+1 = 12
XIII = 10+1+1+1 = 13
XIV = 10+(5-1) = 14
XV = 10+5 = 15

XVI = 10+5+1 = 16
XVII = 10+5+1+1 = 17
XVIII = 10+5+1+1+1 = 18
XIX = (10-1)+10 = 19
XX = 10+10 = 20
XXI = 10+10+1 = 21
XXII = 10+10+1+1 = 22
XXIII = 10+10+1+1+1 = 23
XXIV = 10+10+(5-1) = 24
XXV = 10+10+5 = 25
XXVI = 10+10+5+1 = 26
XXVII = 10+10+5+1+1 = 27
XXVIII = 10+10+5+1+1+1 = 28
XXIX = 10+10+(10-1) = 29
XXX = 10+10+10 = 30

Roman Numerals *(cont.)*

Complete the activities using the information on page 148.

Activity 1: Write the missing Roman numerals.

31 = XXXI	45 =	59 =	73 =	87 =
32 =	46 =	60 = LX	74 = LXXIV	88 =
33 = XXXIII	47 =	61 =	75 =	89 =
34 =	48 = XLVIII	62 =	76 = LXXVI	90 = XC
35 = XXXV	49 = IL	63 =	77 =	91 =
36 =	50 = L	64 =	78 =	92 =
37 =	51 =	65 = LXV	79 =	93 =
38 =	52 =	66 =	80 =	94 =
39 = IXL	53 =	67 =	81 =	95 = XCV
40 = XL	54 =	68 =	82 = LXXXII	96 =
41 = XLI	55 = LV	69 =	83 =	97 =
42 =	56 =	70 = LXX	84 =	98 =
43 =	57 =	71 =	85 =	99 =
44 = XLIV	58 =	72 =	86 =	100 = C

Activity 2: Write your date of birth and telephone number in Arabic numbers and then in Roman numerals. Which system uses the most symbols?

Activity 3: Write the numbers for the hours on this clock face in Roman numerals. Do you have any clocks at home like this?

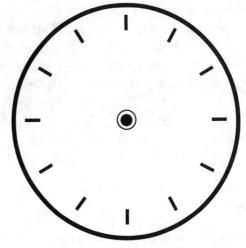

Activity 4: Write the Arabic number equivalent to these Roman numerals.

1. CXLV =
2. CCCLXXXII =
3. DCLIII =
4. DLX =
5. MMXLVII =
6. MMMDXXV =

Activity 5: Write the Roman numeral equivalent to these Arabic numbers.

1. 265 =
2. 483 =
3. 901 =
4. 1,075 =
5. 5,247 =
6. 2,603 =

Plutarc the Painter

Narrators 1–6

Spartus—son

Serena—daughter

Gothum—glassmaker

Avidius—attendant

Plutarc—painter

Brisias—wife

Patric—potter

Martin—mosaic maker

Narrator 1: Rome was a crowded, thriving community of people who worked hard and played hard. Join Plutarc, a local painter, and his family as they venture into town during a typical Roman holiday.

Plutarc: Our Emperor spends enormous funds to keep his people happy so that we will support his decisions. Besides giving free grain to the poor, he sponsors several holidays throughout the year, like this one today. These holidays may be religious festivals to honor one of our many gods or simply days for pleasure and entertainment at the theater, Colosseum, or racetrack. At least one-third of the year is devoted to holidays.

Brisias: And if we're going to make it on time for the chariot races today, we'd better get started on our errands. Our first stop is at your shop to pick up Martin. I'm anxious to see the **mosaic** for the Emperor's entryway. Martin is such a good artist, I'm sure it will be beautiful.

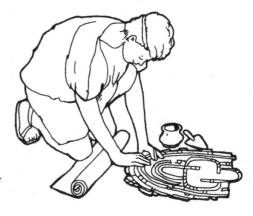

Narrator 1: Plutarc is also an artist, a painter who has earned quite a reputation among the wealthy. He paints frescoes to decorate the walls inside their villas. Early Roman painters painted false columns and masonry blocks inside homes to make the walls look three dimensional. Then they often added pictures of mythological scenes, landscapes, or other things. Huge murals were painted in some homes to give the illusion of spaciousness. Plutarc is especially talented at painting false windows and doorways. He creates "views" out of windowless walls, using perspective, shadowing, and overlapping. Many times you cannot tell the real window from the false!

Plutarc: Here we are. Greetings, Martin. Are you ready to take in a bath and some sport? First show Brisias your latest mosaic for the Emperor. Then we'll leave the ladies to finish their shopping.

Martin: It's been three months of hard work, but I am finished with the main **mural**. The Emperor wanted an elaborate picture showing his latest military conquest. I have only the border pattern to complete. Making a mosaic takes great skill and patience. Even though I have many apprentices working for me to cut, sort, and lay the colored bits of stone, pottery, and glass, I still must supervise their every move. We use several different techniques, depending on the design of the mosaic. Sometimes we mark the pattern directly onto the cement floor and then lay the pieces in the wet mortar, a small section at a time. Other times we make sections of the mosaic in the shop by gluing the stones upside down onto a cloth. Then we can take the entire finished panel to the site and lay it in the fresh mortar. The cloth is soaked and peeled off once the mortar and stones have set. After the entire mosaic is finished we will grind the surface smooth and polish it. I must say, my tired knees will welcome the baths today!

Plutarc the Painter *(cont.)*

Brisias: We'll meet you men later at the Circus Maximus. Come, Serena, we must stop at the potter's stall and the glassmakers while the men enjoy their baths. I want to order a new platter from Patric since the old one was broken at our last dinner party. Sometimes our slaves can be so clumsy! Here we are. Hello, Patric. My daughter and I want to select a new platter. Can you show us some?

Patric: Gladly. Although my pottery is mass-produced, I think you'll find the craftsmanship superb. The Samian factories in France also do fine work with their special red pottery. Come, let me show you some of my best platters. My potters are very skilled at controlling the big kilns precisely so that the glaze is not cracked or cloudy. Which do you prefer?

Serena: I like the plain rectangular platter because it will go nicely with our other serving pieces. Mother, may I go watch the **glassblowing** while you pay? It's magic the way they turn a bubble into such fine vessels.

Brisias: Yes, yes, run along. I will be there shortly. Use your best manners. What do I owe you for the platter, Patric? I will have to pick it up tomorrow. We're on our way to the races right now.

Narrator 2: Glassblowing was an important new craft in Ancient Roman times. Although ways of making glass had been known for centuries, the idea of blowing glass bubbles and shaping them was relatively new. This technology allowed glass to move from being an expensive luxury to being an everyday material used for items in most homes. Sometimes broken glass was collected for recycling, just as it is today.

Gothum: Stand back, Serena, so that you aren't burned. You have been here so often to watch that perhaps today you can persuade your mother to buy you a trinket. Over here are a few of the mass-produced bowls and bottles. Some have bands of colored glass and gold, while others have intricate textures made by the different molds. These Portland vases are for the Emperor himself. They were made by layering white glass over a blue core. The white layer was then carved away, leaving the delicate scene of foliage and figures on a blue background. Because of the time, skill, and precision involved, these are very expensive.

Plutarc the Painter *(cont.)*

Brisias: Serena, you may choose a cosmetic flask today as a treat. I must try to talk your father into buying some new cups, since our bronze ones give the wine a bad aftertaste. Hurry, because we still need to stop at the food stall to eat.

Narrator 3: While Serena and her mother finished shopping, the men enjoyed a relaxing afternoon at the **public bath house**. Ancient Roman bath houses were not just places to get clean. They served as centers where men socialized, exercised, and played games. Women usually bathed in the morning or at separate bath houses. The buildings were grand affairs able to accommodate thousands of people. They had an exercise yard or hall and changing rooms that led to a series of progressively hotter bathing chambers. These chambers consisted of either dry heat, like a sauna, or steam. The Ancient Romans believed that the heat would sweat impurities out of their bodies. Then they would dip into refreshing pools of cool water. The final pool was cold to help close the pores of the skin.

Avidius: Gentlemen, I am your attendant. Here are wooden clogs to protect your feet from the hot floor tiles. This olive oil will cleanse your bodies, especially if you use the strigils to scrape the oil, sweat, and dirt from your skin. Please leave your clothes here in the changing room.

Plutarc: Thank you, Avidius. We won't do the full regimen today, because we are on our way to the chariot races. I think we will bathe and then have a massage and meal. Spartus might enjoy some training today, but Martin and I would like to chat about the races and make some wagers with friends. We will call for you when we need you. For now, please attend to Spartus. He tends to spend more time wrestling and less time getting clean.

Narrator 4: Many wealthy Romans brought along slaves to carry towels and bathing implements. These slaves would help the men bathe while they discussed the latest gossip. Attendants could also be hired for a small fee. Ball games and other exercises were played in the gymnasium or out in a yard. The less energetic could purchase food and drinks from vendors and sit in the shade to play gambling games with boards of dice. Some bath houses had extensive libraries and reading rooms, as well as beautiful gardens. Some days bathers could enjoy a poetry recital or music concert.

Martin: I hear we may have some music today. I fancy the **lyre** of Apollo or the reed pipes of Pan the shepherd god. Some of these modern pipes, flutes, and horns are so loud they are only proper in the Arena itself.

Plutarc the Painter *(cont.)*

Plutarc: My brother is a musician, as you know, and has been attempting to learn the double pipes. He has been honored by being asked to play the **cornu**, or spiral horn, today to announce the opening of the races.

Narrator 5: Roman music was adopted mainly from the Greeks. The Romans did invent brass instruments such as horns to use for military and ceremonial purposes. They held music competitions that drew participants from all over the Roman Empire.

Spartus: Father, are you finished? I am most anxious to get to the racetrack. The chariot races are by far my favorite **ludi**, or holiday games, put on by the Emperor. Many boys enjoy the battles at the **Colosseum**, but I think they have become far too bloody.

Martin: I agree. Originally the **gladiator** battles had a religious purpose and were fought at the funerals of great men to honor the deceased. Over time, the spectacles have become a way to entertain the public. The mornings are filled with mock hunts. The Emperor spends a vast portion of our taxes to ship lions, tigers, jaguars, bears, and wild deer and boar from all over the Empire to be slaughtered in the Arena. Sometimes it is the animals who do the killing, when they are put in the Arena with defenseless criminals. I hear some Christians were also executed in this manner, although there is no record of this atrocity happening here at the Colosseum in Rome.

Plutarc: The fighting is so bloody that they must stop at midday to remove bodies and spread fresh sand on the Arena floor. Sometimes clowns provide light entertainment, or there might be public executions. Of course, the main attraction is the gladiator battles. Usually these are single fights between different types of gladiators, but sometimes the Arena is turned into an all-out battlefield! I favor the nimble **retiarius**, armed only with a weighted net and trident, to the heavily armed **murmillo** and the spear-throwing **velites**.

Spartus: Most of these battles are to the death, but sometimes when a gladiator is wounded he can appeal to the crowd for mercy from the Emperor. If he fought bravely, the crowd may signal "thumbs up" to allow the Emperor to let the man live. Other times the crowd will turn their thumbs down, and the gladiator will be killed. Most gladiators are common criminals or slaves hoping to win their freedom. But some are trained to compete well. There are those who think the life of a gladiator is glamorous and romantic because winning a battle also wins the hearts of the ladies. Some men even volunteer for the job.

Martin: Even though many citizens enjoy the bloodshed, many more are growing bored with the battles and crave novelty. The last competition had women gladiators and even midget warriors from Africa. I hear the Emperor is planning to fill the arena with water and conduct mock sea battles for the next holiday! What will they think of next?

Plutarc the Painter *(cont.)*

Plutarc: My goodness, look at the time on the sundial! Brisias will have my head if we're late for the opening ceremonies. Quick, let's go.

Narrator 6: All over the Roman Empire people headed to racetracks, called circuses, to watch the chariots race. The greatest racetrack of all was the Circus Maximus in Rome. It seated up to 250,000 people.

Serena: Over here, Father! We just have time to find our seats before the opening ceremonies. I do so like attending the races, for it is the only **ludi** where our whole family may sit together. Even at the **theater**, Mother and I must sit in the back. It's silly to think we might swoon over an actor or a gladiator if we sit too close!

Brisias: Still, I enjoy the theater more. The all-male cast plays all of the roles. Most of our plays are Greek favorites translated into Latin, although lately there have been a few new Roman comedies that have created quite an impression on the public. Most of the plays have lost their religious emphasis and are now put on for competitions and simple entertainment. Roman actors have created a new type of performance called **pantomime**, which incorporates dancing and music to tell a story without speaking.

Spartus: But nothing matches the excitement of the chariot races! The chariots are lightweight to travel at top speeds. Usually they are pulled by four horses and guided by charioteers who are brave, young, and strong. The reins of the horses are tied around the charioteers' waists so that they can't be dropped, but if one topples over the poor driver can't get loose and is dragged on the ground. There are few rules, and many times chariots collide attempting to force opponents off the track!

Plutarc: I, too, look forward to an exciting race. There is my brother now, leading the opening procession. I hope this will be one of our finest Roman holidays yet!

Vocabulary and Comprehension

Write the following words on the chalkboard for students to copy into their vocabulary books. Remind students to define and illustrate each word.

mural	lyre	gladiator	pantomime
mosaic	cornu	retiarius	theater
glassblowing	ludi	murmillo	
public bath house	Colosseum	velites	

Use all or some of the following questions for whole-class discussion, small-group work, or individual assessment. Allow students to refer back to the story while working.

1. What are some types of art and entertainment Ancient Romans practiced and enjoyed? (*Fresco paintings of murals, scenes, and false windows; floor mosaics; pottery; glass-blowing; sculptures at temples and other public buildings; music; dance; theater/drama.*)

2. Describe some types of ludi, or Roman holidays. (*Religious festivals honoring the gods, drama and music competitions, races at the circus, gladiator battles and mock hunts at the Colosseum or local arena.*)

3. How is a trip to the Roman baths similar to and different from visiting a famous spa today? How is it different? (*They both have treatments to cleanse the body and relax; both offer rooms with dry heat or steam to make you sweat; both have attendants; and both offer massages, food, and entertainment. The Roman baths were free to all people, allowing different classes to intermingle. Some famous modern spas are very expensive and, therefore, exclusively for the wealthy.*)

4. What is the difference between the Colosseum and the Circus Maximus? (*The Colosseum was a large open arena or amphitheater where the gladiator battles took place. The Circus Maximus was a large racetrack built exclusively for chariot races.*)

5. Why did the Emperor create more exotic and bloody battles? What does this tell you about Ancient Roman culture? (*The public grew bored with watching men and beasts fight. When they became used to that level of violence, they craved ever more brutal and spectacular exhibitions. Accept reasonable answers for the other part.*)

6. How are these Roman sports similar to sports and other forms of entertainment today? (*The fans root for and bet on their favorites; chariot races are similar to horse racing today; men battling wild beasts is similar to watching the animal tamers at the circus; boxing and other sports are similar to the gladiator battles, etc.*)

Make a Mosaic

Have students create paper mosaics using techniques developed by the Romans. Students will create individual mosaic panels that combine to form a large mosaic to display on a bulletin board.

Preparing for the lesson:

1. Reproduce a Mosaic Panel (page 157) for each student onto gray construction paper. Trim the edges so that each panel is a square.

2. Cut ½" (1 cm) squares of white and at least four other colors of construction paper. Place the squares into containers for students to share.

3. Gather glue and scissors for each student.

4. Gather pictures of mosaics from books, and make a sample mosaic panel yourself as a sample.

Teaching the lesson:

1. Display the examples of mosaics. Note that many Roman mosaics were intricate portraits and scenes created on the floors of homes, temples, and other public buildings. Ask students if they have ever seen a mosaic and what it looked like. Today, most mosaics are created from pieces of tile set into mortar to form pictures and designs. This technique is similar to the Roman mosaics.

2. Tell students that sometimes the mosaics were created on smaller panels and then combined to form a larger mosaic. This is what they will do as a class, only instead of tile and mortar they will use paper and glue.

3. Distribute the Mosaic Panels, glue, scissors, and paper squares to students. (You may want students to push their desks together to share materials easily.) Have students write their names on the back of the panel. Tell students to use only white squares on the sections labeled "white" on their patterns. They may use any color and pattern on the rest. The white border will help incorporate all of the panels so that it looks like one large mosaic when completed. Show your completed sample.

4. Encourage students to cover only a small area with glue, then cover the glue with colored squares. The squares should be close together but not touching or overlapping. They may use scissors to cut the squares to a different shape to make it fit the pattern outline. All portions of the mosaic panel should be covered with paper when finished.

5. Let the mosaic panels dry. Then arrange them all on a bulletin board to form a large square or rectangle. Use strips of white paper to make a border around the entire mosaic. If bulletin board space is not available, line them above the chalkboard as a border.

Make a Mosaic *(cont.)*

Mosaic Panel

The Barbarian Invasions

By A.D. 200 the future of Rome was uncertain. The Roman Empire was in decline as a result of a variety of problems. However, one of the major factors was invasions from tribes of barbarians. The barbarians were people who came from areas beyond the territory of the Roman Empire. There were four main tribes involved in these invasions over about 300 years. They were the Goths (Visigoths and Ostrogoths) and Vandals from Germany, the Huns from Asia, and the Franks from northeast of Gaul (France). These tribes were attracted by the prosperous cities and plentiful farm land. The Romans found these nomads rough and uncivilized, but they admired their courage and simple lifestyle.

The Visigoths traveled south from Sweden around A.D. 200 and moved through Germany to settle in Dacia (Romania), north of the Roman Provinces in Greece. Around A.D. 350 the Visigoths were attacked and defeated by the much-feared Huns, who were making their way westward from Asia. By this time the Roman Empire had been reorganized into the Eastern Byzantine Empire and the Western Roman Empire. The Roman military was weakened and unprepared for invasion.

For the Visigoths to protect themselves from the Huns, they had to cross the Danube River into the Roman Empire. In A.D. 376 the Roman emperor gave the tribe permission to do this, because he hoped to hire the Visigoths to work for the Roman army. This proved a tragic mistake. The Visigoths began to sack and pillage Roman cities.

The Visigoths lived in several small tribes. Each tribe had a leader, and tribal order was based on devout loyalty to this leader. The Visigoths were nomadic, so they did not live in permanent houses or have many possessions. A person's worth was based on bravery rather than wealth. They had a few simple laws that were enforced by the leader. Guilt was determined by a test rather than in court. For example, an accused person might be made to walk on fire. If his wounds healed quickly, he was found innocent. If they didn't, he was guilty. This form of justice was called trial by ordeal. Today we often refer to somebody doing something extremely difficult as a "trial by fire."

Like the early Romans, the Visigoths practiced polytheism. But they worshipped their gods in forests, not temples. Sometimes animals and humans were sacrificed, and they used certain rituals to predict the future. Since they were nomadic, the Visigoths were hunters and gatherers. They did have cattle and got milk from them. Food was cooked in simple undecorated clay pots.

Since the men were often away in battle, women played an important role in the domestic, political, and spiritual life of the tribe. Women were responsible for feeding and clothing everyone. They planted crops, cooked, washed, brewed beer, and tended to the sick. Although they did not go off to war themselves, they fought strongly to defend their homes. In many tribes, powerful women known as prophets or priestesses helped make political decisions and led religious ceremonies.

The Barbarian Invasions *(cont.)*

A new Visigoth leader named Alaric emerged. He led the Visigoths as they conquered Roman provinces in Greece, overran Gaul, and began to move towards Rome itself. Alaric demanded a ransom to spare Rome. When he did not get one, he attacked the city.

The various barbarian tribes became very powerful. They marched through Gaul and entered Spain. By A.D. 439 they had reached Carthage in Northern Africa. Attila the Hun defeated the last Roman general in Gaul in A.D. 451. A second Germanic tribe called the Vandals sacked Rome several years later. They took great pleasure in destroying many of the buildings that Alaric had left standing. Today we use the word "vandalism" to describe this type of destruction of property.

In A.D. 467 the last emperor of the Western Roman Empire, Romulus Augustulus, was defeated, bringing to an end the greatest empire the world had ever seen. Soon after, other barbarian tribes spread into Europe. The Franks conquered and renamed Gaul (France), and the Angles and Saxons renamed Britain (England). Europe entered a 500-year period of decline known as the Dark Age. Trade was disrupted by warfare, the education system broke down, and day-to-day survival was the main concern of most people. The Christian church began to develop religious communities called monasteries throughout Europe. The monasteries were centers for learning, and they preserved much of the history of Greco-Roman civilizations in books.

Although the Eastern Byzantine Empire also experienced wars throughout this time, it survived the barbarian attacks and remained intact for another thousand years. By A.D. 634 the armies of Islam had begun to invade the Eastern Empire. Religious wars raged until the Ottoman Turks conquered Constantinople in 1453. The great Roman Empire was gone.

Barbarian Invasions of the Roman Empire

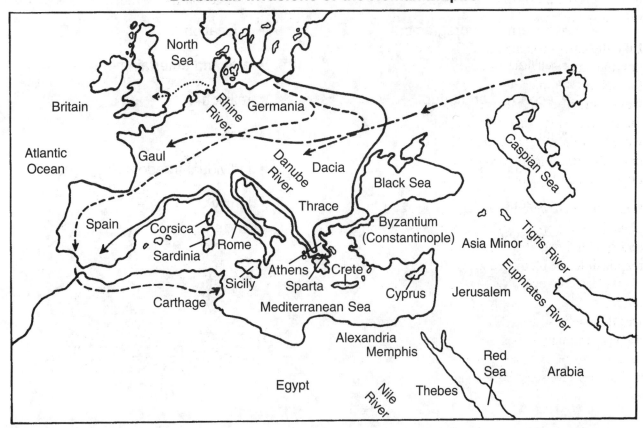

The Fall of the Roman Empire— A Lesson for Today?

In the 18th century, Edward Gibbons wrote *The Decline and Fall of the Roman Empire*. Before and since, historians and others have expressed theories and presented analyses that offer explanations for why the mighty empire fell. Most believe that it was not the result of one particular factor or event, but rather a slow and cumulative process that involved many different factors which, combined, led to the decline and fall of the Roman Empire.

Why does it matter to us today why an ancient, powerful empire ended? An oft-repeated phrase goes something like this: "Those who do not learn from the past are doomed to repeat it." What do you think that means? By examining the reasons that contributed to Rome's decline, perhaps we can evaluate the state of our own civilization. Are we, the most powerful nation today, making the same mistakes as the Ancient Romans? If so, what are they and how can we prevent the same fate from befalling our nation?

Brainstorm a list of things that helped cause the decline of the Roman Empire. Divide into groups to research and write a comparison of what role these things played in Ancient Rome and what role they play in our society today. Be prepared to present your findings to the class, and develop some personal theories about what could cause the decline and fall of the United States of America.

Choose one of the topics below or something else that you feel added to the erosion of Ancient Roman society and that may also be negatively affecting our own today.

- government structure
- government programs
- military
- economy and trade
- jobs
- social class
- disease
- morality

- foreign invasion
- education
- arts and entertainment
- religion
- race
- individual freedom and rights
- family

Ancient Rome—Assessment

Matching: Match each term to its definition:

_____ 1. The mountain range that extends the length of the Roman peninsula.

_____ 2. The civilization that was conquered by the Romans and contributed greatly to their religion, architecture, theater, literature, and education.

_____ 3. The major river used to transport goods to and from Rome.

_____ 4. The legendary founder and first king of Rome.

_____ 5. The North African territory that fought Rome in the Punic Wars.

_____ 6. The sea that lies at the base of the boot of Italy, near Sicily.

_____ 7. The two main agricultural exports of Rome.

_____ 8. The capital of the Roman Empire until the reign of Constantine.

_____ 9. The sea that separates Italy from Greece.

_____ 10. The first civilized inhabitants of Rome, whose contributions included the arch and alphabet.

_____ 11. The people living in central Italy who gave the Roman Empire its language.

A. Romulus **B.** Etruscans **C.** Latins **D.** Greeks **E.** Adriatic Sea **F.** Ionion Sea **G.** Tiber River
H. Apennine Mountains **I.** olive and grape products **J.** Rome **K.** Carthage

Fill in the Blanks: Fill in the blank with the name of the appropriate leader:

Julius Caesar   Augustus Caesar   Nero   Cleopatra   Constantine

12. He changed the future of the Roman Empire by naming Christianity as the official Roman religion. _____ moved the capital from Rome to Constantinople.

13. _____ was a bold military general who craved power. He won a civil war against Rome and made himself dictator. When the Senate decided he had gained too much power and was a threat to the Republic, they had him assassinated.

14. After the death of his father, _____ expanded the Empire and began a prosperous period known as the Pax Romana. He was a popular leader and made great contributions to Roman wealth and culture.

15. _____ was not a popular Emperor, and some believed that he may have started the great fire of Rome himself so he could blame it on the Christians. He punished the Christians in cruel ways and eventually committed suicide.

16. _____ ruled Rome from Egypt. She consulted with Julius Caesar and then Mark Antony after Caesar's death. She and Mark Antony committed suicide out of love.

Matching

Indicate the social class described by placing each letter in the appropriate box(es):

17. Upper-class Romans ☐ ☐ ☐ ☐ ☐ ☐

18. Middle- and Lower-class Romans ☐ ☐ ☐ ☐ ☐ ☐

A. could hold a government, religious, or military office

B. attended a Roman Holiday at the Circus Maximus

C. went to school

D. comprised the majority of Roman society

E. received free grain from the Emperor

F. could go to the public baths

G. owned personal slaves

H. wore togas

I. lived in the insulae

J. dined in the triclinium

Ancient Rome—Assessment *(cont.)*

On the blanks, write the letter of the answer that correctly completes each statement.

_____ 19. The early form of Roman government in which two consuls were advised by a Senate was

      A. an oligarchy   B. a Republic   C. a democracy

_____ 20. The wealthy upper-class citizens who could make all decisions in the Senate were the

      A. patricians   B. plebeians   C. Latins

_____ 21. The plebeians fought for their rights and were able to help document Roman law in

      A. the Ten Commandments   B. Hammurabi's law   C. the Twelve Tablets

_____ 22. Eventually the Republic allowed plebeians and patricians to hold office as Consuls. Each Consul had the ability to stop a ruling of the others. This power is called

      A. supremacy   B. veto   C. tyranny

_____ 23. Early Romans worshipped many gods. This practice is called

      A. gentiles   B. republicanism   C. polytheism

_____ 24. Early Romans were very superstitious. They sacrificed animals at temples and examined their entrails to find

      A. gods   B. disease   C. omens

_____ 25. Jews and Christians referred to the Romans who worshipped Jupiter, Saturn, and Mercury as

      A. pagans   B. heretics   C. Gentiles

_____ 26. Once Christianity became the official religion of the Roman Empire,

      A. all forms of persecution ended   B. the Christians persecuted the Jews   C. the Christians and Jews persecuted the pagans

Essay Questions

Answer each question with complete and detailed sentences. Use the back of the page.

27. How did the geography and location of Italy help the Roman Empire to flourish?

28. How did Roman government change with the introduction of emperors?

29. Why did the Romans persecute the Jews and Christians while allowing other religions to practice freely?

30. Describe at least three factors that contributed to the decline and fall of the Roman Empire.

31. Name at least three lasting contributions of the Ancient Romans.

32. What do you think we can learn from the Ancient Romans so that our civilization won't crumble like theirs did?

Ancient Rome Assessment—Answer Key

Matching

1. H
2. D
3. G
4. A
5. K
6. F

7. I
8. J
9. E
10. B
11. C

Fill in the Blank

12. Constantine
13. Julius Caesar
14. Augustus Caesar
15. Nero
16. Cleopatra

Multiple Choice

17. A, B, C, F, G, H, J
18. B, D, E, F, H, I
19. B
20. A
21. C

22. B
23. C
24. C
25. A
26. C

Essay Questions

27. The united Roman peninsula allowed people to travel easily throughout Italy. The mountains provided protection and the rivers helped transport people and goods. Italy's location in the middle of the Mediterranean region meant they could trade with a variety of people and have easy access to conquer.

28. Once emperors took over the government, the Republic was gone. Although the Senate advised the Emperor, there was no one who could veto his decisions. This meant the Emperor had supreme power. Rome never became democratic.

29. The Jews and the Christians believed in and worshipped only one god. Their laws prohibited them from carrying out the rituals of the Romans. The Romans felt this was a threat to their Empire and tried to force the Jews and Christians to comply. When they refused, the Roman government persecuted them in a variety of ways, including crucifixion, or execution by hanging on a cross. Other religions were willing to accept the Roman ways and also practice their own religion. These people were left alone.

30. Accept a description of any three of the following: barbarian invasions, the spread of Christianity, economic decline, decline of morality, disease, decrease in slavery, growth of government, changes in the military, desire for greater individual freedom.

31. Accept examples of any three of the following: designing and building great cities, roads, architecture, plumbing, legal administration, calendars, coins, entertainment, the arts.

32. Accept reasonable answers.

Literature Connection—Planning Guide

Simulation Roles Chart

Beginning the Literature Simulation (Literature pages appear in paranthesis.)
Time Spiral (4–5)—How Do We Know? (42–43)—Basic Facts About Roman Life (6–7)—Your Map of the Roman World (8–9)—Begin Your New Life Here (10–13)

Government
Law and Order (32–33)—The Army (36–37)

Science and Achievements
City or Country? (16–17)—Sickness and Health (24–25)

Social Structure and Family Life
Your House (14–15)—Your Family (18–19)—Food and Drink (20–21)—Your Clothes (22–23)—Careers (28–29)—Birth, Marriage, and Death (40–41)

Economy and Trade
Travel and Trade (34–35)

Religion
The Gods (38–39)

Education
Education (26–27)

The Arts and Entertainment
Entertainment (30–31)

Preparing to Teach the Literature Lessons

1. Have students make a literature journal by stapling writing paper between construction paper covers before starting the lessons. This provides a way for them to keep a record of their responses to simulation activities. Tell them not to decorate the front cover until the first lesson. Some lessons provide group activities that do not require completion in students' journals.

2. Tell students that they will each assume a role in Ancient Roman society. As you lead them through activities for each section, they will complete the activity in their journals. They must stay in character for the role they have been assigned and make their journal entries as that character.

3. Reproduce the Simulation Roles Chart (page 165). Cut out the role name/description boxes and place them in two containers—one for males and one for females. Tell students that they are all married and have children. Their social class will depend on their occupation (males) or their husband's occupation (females).

4. Have each student draw a role from the appropriate container. This will be their permanent place/occupation in their simulations.

5. After each activity, have students share their journal responses with the class. Discuss with the class how the same events are experienced differently, depending on a person's place in Roman society.

6. After completing all of the literature lessons, reproduce for each student a copy of the fun quiz on page 46 in the literature book to answer the question "Have you Survived?" Allow students to check their own pages as you discuss and tell the correct answers (on page 48 of the literature book). Using the guide on page 48 to let students know their survival rating.

Simulation Roles Chart

Upper-class Male	Middle-class Male	Lower-class Male	Male Slave
high-ranking army general	bridge engineer in Rome	grape farmer	Greek tutor
Upper-class Male	**Middle-class Male**	**Lower-class Male**	**Male Slave**
Aedile—in charge of the markets, public buildings, and holiday games	soldier in the army	crewman on a merchant ship	dig ditches for roads
Upper-class Male	**Middle-class Male**	**Lower-class Male**	**Male Slave**
Senator	landlord of a city tenement	actor	work on a grain farm
Upper-class Male	**Middle-class Male**	**Lower-class Male**	**Male Slave**
wealthy import/export trader	merchant ship captain	plumbing laborer	gladiator
Upper-class Female	**Middle-class Female**	**Lower-class Female**	**Female Slave**
wife of the temple priest of Jupiter	wife of a weapons maker	wife of a laundryman	dressing slave for a noblewoman
Upper-class Female	**Middle-class Female**	**Lower-class Female**	**Female Slave**
wife of a Praetor, or high judge	wife of a cobbler/shoemaker	wife of a chariot racer	cooking slave for a patrician family
Upper-class Female	**Middle-class Female**	**Lower-class Female**	**Female Slave**
wife of a navy admiral	doctor	wife of an olive farmer	cloth weaver
Upper-class Female	**Middle-class Female**	**Lower-class Female**	**Female Slave**
wife of Rome's tax collector	wife of a sculptor/stonemason	run a food stall with your husband	cares for patrician children

Beginning the Literature Simulation

Connection to the Interdisciplinary Unit:

You may wish to reinforce this simulation section with what you previously studied in this unit after its completion, or use it simotaneously with the different sections of the unit. Unit pages have been listed along with literature pages. Corresponding pages are listed.

Introducing the Literature Book:

1. Distribute the literature books and have students review the Time Spiral (pages 4–5). Discuss the important events noted at the beginning of the spiral and their relation to one another. Which of these events have you studied already?

2. Tell students that they will use their literature books, their journals, and information from the unit on Ancient Rome and other resources as they take a journey through time and participate in history. They will respond in their journals as accurately as possible, based on their roles in Ancient Roman society.

3. Direct students to turn to pages 42–43, How Do We Know? Discuss ways that historians can reconstruct the past so we know about ancient civilizations.

4. Have students turn to pages 6–7, Basic Facts About Roman Life. Tell students that they will be learning more about each of these areas. Have students take turns reading the sections aloud to the class.

Beginning the Journals:

1. Have students open their journals and write on the first page the basic information for their simulation: their chosen Roman name, their place in Roman society, their occupation or the occupation of their spouse, and a brief description of their family. A typical journal entry might look like this:

   Greetings, fellow Romans! My name is Felicia and I am a member of the Roman middle-class. I am married to a painter named Hector. We have two children. Our son Hadrian is 13, and our daughter Alexandra is 9.

2. Once students have completed their first journal entry, have them decorate the front cover of their journal, give it a title that includes their assigned role, write their own real name, and draw an appropriate illustration. Example:

   How Would You Survive as a Middle-Class Painter's Wife in Ancient Rome?

   by Suzie Jones

Reading and Discussion:

1. Then have students turn to page 8 in their literature books. Tell them to read pages 8–13 ONLY (Your Map of the Ancient World and Begin Your New Life Here) to get an overview of their simulated life. Allow students time to read and study these pages.

2. Tell students that as you work through the simulations, different roles will require different participation in the activities. At times, the upper-class females may seem to be doing most of the activities; at other times it may be male slaves. Assure them that they will all get an equal chance to actively participate during the simulation.

Class Role Groupings:

1. When you divide the class into four groups, they are: upper- and middle-class males; upper- and middle-class females; lower-class and slave males; lower-class and slave females.

2. When you divide the class into eight groups, they are: upper-class males; middle-class males; upper-class females; middle-class females; lower-class males; slave males; lower-class females; slave females.

Government

Connection to the Interdisciplinary Unit:

This literature section corresponds to pages 30–41 in the unit.

Literature Book:

1. Have students turn in their literature books to pages 32–33, Law and Order. Divide the class into four groups as described at the bottom of page 166.

2. Have the groups read, discuss, and respond in their journals to all of the following that apply to their role.

Journal Response:

A. Describe your or your husband's career in politics. What steps did you or he take to obtain your current position? What are you or he responsible for in the government? Do you or he have any further aspirations?

B. Based on your social class, what is your opinion of the Roman code of law? Do you feel you are protected and well represented? Why or why not?

C. Describe what happened on the last visit to the tax collector. How did it affect your family? What is your opinion of the taxes?

D. A member of your family has been accused of a crime and given a punishment. Describe who did what crime, the punishment, and how it all has affected your family.

Simulation Activity:

Have your class simulate a court case. Allow the upper-and middle-class students to act as the judge, jury, and lawyers. Assign roles for the trial. Choose one lower-class student to accuse another lower class student of a crime associated with their occupations. Have both the accuser and the accused enlist the aid of a lawyer.

On trial day have the accused brought into court and the charges against him or her read. Have the judge swear in the jury and listen to both sides of the case. The lawyers, the accused, and the accuser have an opportunity to speak. The jury votes, and, if necessary, the judge announces a punishment.

Discussion:

Have students share their journal responses with the class. Discuss how government affects the different social classes. Was Roman law fair for all? Were some seen as above the law? Were some given special treatment? Was punishment harsh or fair? How could/does our society today benefit from some elements of Roman law?

Government *(cont.)*

Connection to the Interdisciplinary Unit:

This literature section corresponds to pages 42–48 of the unit.

Literature Book:

1. Have students open their literature books to pages 36–37, The Army. Divide the class into four groups.

2. Have the groups read the information, discuss, and respond in their journals to all of the following that apply to their role.

Journal Response:

A. You or your husband have chosen a career in the Roman army or navy. Describe this career. What steps were taken to achieve this position? What responsibilities do you or he have? Do you or he have any future goals related to the military?

B. A legion has just come into town to protect you from invaders. Describe your feelings and how the legion coming has affected your job and family.

C. You admire the brave soldiers and their modern equipment. Draw and label a picture in your journal describing a legionnaire. If you are in the military yourself, draw and label a picture of your uniform.

D. You are a smith who makes armor and weapons for the military. Describe some of the things you make. How does it feel to have this job?

Discussion:

Have students share their journal responses with the class. What was it like to be in the military? How was Ancient Roman military life similar to military life today? How was it different?

Science and Achievements

Connection to the Interdisciplinary Unit:

This literature section corresponds to pages 75–81 of the unit.

Literature Book:

1. On the chalkboard list the titles and page numbers for the two literature book sections that students will use for this simulation: City or Country?, pages 16–17, and Sickness and Health, pages 24–25.
2. Divide the class into four groups.
3. Have the groups read the information, discuss, and respond in their journals to all of the following that apply to their role.

Journal Response for City or Country?, pages 16–17:

A. Describe a walk through your city. What buildings do you see? What hazards might you encounter? Did you help to fund any of the public buildings?

B. You or your husband helped build this fine city. Describe your contributions and how it feels to see your work being used every day by your fellow citizens.

C. You live on a farm. Describe your life there and the jobs you perform. Do you like your daily routine? What would you change if you could?

Discussion:

Have students share their journal responses with the class. Talk about how cities in Ancient Rome were built and how that differs from construction today. What are some of the contributions Romans made to modern building practices or styles? If you haven't completed Roman Architecture (page 79 of the unit), you may wish to do so now.

Journal Response for Sickness and Health, pages 24–25:

A. You are married to a fuller, who cleans clothes. Describe your husband's duties and your feelings about being married to him. Do you help with the family business?

B. Regardless of your social class all citizens could attend the public baths after a hard day of work. (Women took their baths in the mornings or during special hours.) Describe a visit to the baths. What did you do there?

C. As a slave you have been asked to attend the baths with your master or mistress. What were your duties while at the baths? What are your feelings about these duties?

D. You have taken ill. What are the options available to assist your recovery? Describe your symptoms and what you do. Do you consult a doctor? Do you see the chemist or go to a temple? What is done about your illness? What happens to you?

E. You are a doctor in Ancient Rome. How did you become a doctor? What are some of your duties and responsibilities? How do you feel about your occupation?

Discussion:

Have students share their journal responses with the class. Why do you think the baths were open to all social classes while everything else in Roman society was limited? How has medicine improved? How has it remained the same?

Social Structure and Family Life

Connection to the Interdisciplinary Unit:

This literature section corresponds to pages 82–95 of the unit.

Literature Book:

1. On the chalkboard list the following titles and pages from the literature book: Your House, 14–15; Your Family, 18–19; Food and Drink, 20–21; Your Clothes, 22-23; Careers, 28–29; Birth, Marriage, and Death, 40–41.

2. Divide the class into eight groups as described at the bottom of page 166 in the unit.

3. Have the groups read and discuss the information and respond in their journals to several sections of the literature books that apply to this simulation. You may wish to present this longer simulation section over two or more days.

4. Have groups work through these sections together as they read, discuss, and respond in their journals.

5. Have students share their journal entries with the class after each category is completed. Discuss how life varied for individuals based on their social class. How is this still true today?

Journal Response to Your House, pages 14–15:

A. Draw a label picture and then describe your home. What are the benefits and drawbacks to your home?

B. What is your opinion of your landlord if you live in a city apartment or tenement? What are your responsibilities and feelings if you are the landlord?

Journal Response to Your Family, pages 18–19:

A. Describe a day in the life of your family.

B. How did you get to be in this social class? Describe your family heritage.

C. You are someone who cares for a wealthy family. Describe your responsibilities and feelings as you carry out these tasks.

Journal Response to Food and Drink, pages 20–21:

A. You are someone who prepares food for other Romans. Describe your tasks and your feelings about this responsibility. Then share your favorite recipe and tell how the dish is prepared.

B. As a lower-class Roman or slave you eat simple meals. What did you eat today for breakfast, lunch, and dinner? Who prepared the food, and where did you eat?

C. Upper-class Romans threw lavish dinner parties. Occasionally, friends from the middle-class were also invited to join them, although they were served different food. You have been invited to one of these dinner parties in honor of visiting clients from Egypt. Describe the evening, your meals, and activities as an upper- or middle-class Roman.

Social Structure and Family Life *(cont.)*

Journal Response to Your Clothes, pages 22–23:

A. Draw a picture of how you would look in Ancient Rome. Label each article of clothing, jewelry, make-up, or hairstyle. Give as many interesting details as possible.

B. Describe some fashionable treatments you use to care for your hair or skin.

C. You or your husband are responsible for clothing the Romans by weaving cloth, making shoes, or helping them dress. Describe your daily tasks and feelings.

Journal Response to Careers, pages 28–29:

A. You or your husband have an occupation in Roman society. How did you or he get into this occupation? Share some interesting facts about your work.

B. As a female in Roman society you have many freedoms and responsibilities. Describe your daily routine. Do you work at home taking care of the house and children? Do you help your husband at his business? Are you so wealthy that your slaves do all of the work? Are you so poor that you have very few privileges?

C. Slaves were treated in a variety of ways in Ancient Rome. Describe your master and how you are treated. Do you think you will earn your freedom? Why or why not?

Journal Response to Birth, Marriage, and Death, pages 40–41:

A. You remember fondly the birth of your eldest child. Describe the day, your feelings, and the events surrounding this birth.

B. Another memorable event was your marriage. Describe the events and your feelings at this joyous occasion.

C. Unfortunately, your paterfamilias has become gravely ill. He is expected to die soon, and you have been put in charge of planning his funeral. What arrangements will you make? Will he be cremated or his body placed in a tomb?

Simulation Activity:

Lead a class protest pitting the wealthy against the poor. Have the upper-class students get together to describe why they deserve their status. Have them describe the benefits they offer society and their burden of supporting the poor and enslaved. Have the middle-class, lower-class, and slave classes describe their grievances against the rich. Have them argue the right to work their way up the social ladder. What benefits do they offer society as the bulk of the population?

Economy and Trade

Connection to the Interdisciplinary Unit:

This literature section corresponds to pages 96–102 of the unit.

Literature Book:

1. Have students open their literature books to pages 34–35, Travel and Trade. Divide the class into four groups.
2. Have the groups read and discuss the information and respond in their journals to all of the following that apply to their role.

Journal Response:

A. You have a career in trading, whether it be a wealthy businessman, ship captain, or crewman on a merchant ship. Describe what it is that you trade, where it came from, and how it got to Rome. Have you had any adventures during your travels? Describe your most harrowing experience.
B. You are someone working in the military to keep the roads and sea safe for travel. Describe an event in which you saved some travelers.
C. You helped to build thousands of miles of roads for the Roman Empire. Describe the process for making the roads and your feelings about your work.
D. Your family (or the family that you work for) has saved enough money to visit relatives in another part of the Empire. What plans will you make for the trip? Where are you going; who are you visiting; and why are you making the journey? How will you get there?

Discussion:

Have students share their journal entries with the class. Why was travel easy during the Pax Romana? What benefits did the upper class have for travel? How has travel improved today? Do we have any perils of travel today like they had in Ancient Rome?

Religion

Connection to the Interdisciplinary Unit:

This literature section corresponds to pages 103–106 of the unit.

Literature Book:

1. Have students open their literature books to pages 38–39, The Gods. Divide the class into four groups.
2. Have the groups read and discuss the information, and respond in their journals to all of the following questions that apply to their role.

Journal Response:

A. Your husband is a high official at the temple of Jupiter. Describe his tasks and how it makes you feel to be married to such a man.
B. Describe the daily worship of your family. What superstitions do you follow?
C. You are a slave during the celebration of Saturnalia. What happens during this festival and how does it feel to be free?

Discussion:

Have students share their journal responses with the class. How do Ancient Roman superstitions compare to those we have today? What do you think about superstition? What do you think about faith?

Education

Connection to the Interdisciplinary Unit:

This literature section corresponds with pages 137–149 of the unit.

Literature Book:

1. Have students open their literature books to pages 26–27, Education. Divide the class into four groups.

2. Have the groups read and discuss the information and respond in their journals to all of the following that apply to their role.

Journal Response:

A. As a Greek tutor, or pedagogue, you have many responsibilities. Describe a day of work as a tutor. What lessons do you teach? How do you maintain discipline with your students? How does the wealthy family treat you since you are their slave? Do you like being a tutor? Why or why not?

B. Since you are wealthy, your children will go to school. Describe what school is like for them. At what age do they attend? What will they learn? What career choices do you want them to make?

C. If you have a son, he will have a ceremony to mark his entrance into manhood. Describe this ceremony and how it makes you feel to see your son grow up.

D. You are an upper-or middle-class family with a daughter. She has been chosen to become a Vestal Virgin. What does this mean? How does this make you feel?

E. Since you are from the middle class, are from the lower class, or are a slave, your children cannot go to school. What will they do instead? How does this make you feel? What aspirations do you have for the future of your children?

F. As a mother it is your responsibility to raise the girls in your family. Describe what their education will be like at home. What are you preparing them for?

Discussion:

Have students share their journal responses with the class. How did your education vary depending on your social status? How did this keep people from moving up the social ladder and improving their lives? How has modern public education for all children improved one's ability to become successful regardless of social class? Why do you think some students don't take advantage of this opportunity today and instead cut classes?

Simulation Activity:

Divide the class into boys and girls. Have each group prepare a short presentation describing their lives and opportunities depending on their social class and gender. What special activities are reserved only for boys? Only for girls? How does it feel to be a boy or girl in Ancient Rome?

The Arts and Entertainment

Connection to the Interdisciplinary Unit:

This literature section corresponds to pages 150–157 of the unit.

Literature Book:

1. Have students open their literature books to pages 30–31, Entertainment. Divide the class into four groups.

2. Have the groups read and discuss the information and respond in their journals to all of the following that apply to their role.

Journal Response:

A. You or your husband is responsible for entertaining the Roman public with chariot races and gladiator battles during the holiday games. Describe what you do. Why is this work so dangerous? Did you or he chose this profession? What are your feelings about leading this life? What was your most memorable battle or race? Why was it so memorable?

B. You are an actor who has been hired to perform at the next festival. Describe what your job is like. What preparations must be made before the festival? Who can be an actor? How is a play performed?

C. Today has been declared a holiday, and the Emperor has provided some entertainment. What are you going to see? Describe the event and what you do.

Discussion:

Have students share their journal responses with the class. Why do you think the Romans celebrated in such ways? How do these activities relate to modern-day entertainment? What are your feelings about violence in entertainment?

Role Chart/Schedule for Classroom Simulation of a Circus Maximus (page 175)

Opening Procession	
Gladiator Battle:	Gladiator 1 _____ vs. Gladiator 2 _____
Chariot Race:	Charioteer 1 _____ Horses _____, _____ vs. Charioteer 2 _____ Horses _____, _____
Gladiator Battle:	Gladiator 3 _____ vs. Gladiator 4 _____
Intermission:	Dancers _____, _____, _____, _____, _____, _____, _____
Chariot Race:	Charioteer 3 _____ Horses _____, _____ vs. Charioteer 4 _____ Horses _____, _____
Gladiator Battle:	Gladiator 5 _____ vs. Gladiator 6 _____
Chariot Race:	Charioteer 5 _____ Horses _____, _____ vs. Charioteer 6 _____ Horses _____, _____
Final Gladiator Battle:	winners of the three battles _____, _____, _____
Final Chariot Race:	winners of the three races _____, _____, _____
Royal Executioner:	_____

Create a Circus Maximus

Allow students to create a Circus Maximus for an Ancient Roman holiday.

Preparing for the lesson:

1. If you have not shown the class such movies as *Ben Hur* and *Sparticus*, you may wish to let them watch the chariot race and gladiator battle from each.

2. Make a chart (see page 174) showing the various roles with student's names and what they will participate in.

3. Try to get a portable public address system so you can call out the events and announce the names of the participants.

4. Gather a tape player and Roman music to play during the opening procession and the battles. (You may wish to tape music from *Ben Hur* over and over so you don't have to rewind the tape during the festivities.)

5. Write each student's name on a separate, small piece of paper and mix them all thoroughly in a container.

6. Set aside part of each day for at least a week to allow students time to work together and practice their parts.

7. Set a day and time for the Circus Maximus, and invite guests to watch, if you wish.

Teaching the lesson:

1. Tell students that they will participate in a Roman holiday if they will all agree to play fairly and not hurt each other. Have them all raise their hands to agree.

2. Display the chart and describe the parts available; then draw names from the container, allowing each student to choose the part he or she wants to sign up for. Remind chariot teams that the two horses should be strong and fast and the rider small and light. Write the names in the appropriate places on your chart.

3. Allow students time to research and prepare creative costumes and props. Have them practice their dance routines, battles, and chariot pulls.

   Clothing: Wear togas over school clothes (T-shirts and shorts). Hold the corner of a sheet or large piece of fabric at one shoulder, wrap the fabric around the body once, and tie the corners together at the shoulder. Sandals, jewelry, and make-up might also be worn. Men might comb their hair forward; women might wear buns, curls, or braids.

   Gladiators: Make and wear armor for chest, legs, and arms. Create a helmet and weapons. The battles will be held inside the arena.

   Chariots: Chariots must be DRAGGED—no wheels or sled bars. Create a chariot that is sturdy and able to go around corners without tipping over. The races will be around the outside of the arena.

4. To set up for the event and form the arena, have students arrange chairs in a large circle on a flat area of the school grounds.

5. Have guests take their seats, start the music, and begin the procession with dancers; the emperor (teacher); the gladiators; and the charioteers. As Emperor, welcome everyone and lead the festivities.

6. If foul play is seen during any race or battle, call the culprit in front of you. Describe the offense and allow the culprit to beseech the spectators for mercy. Have the audience show "thumbs up" or thumbs down." If the verdict is "thumbs down" have the Royal Executioner dispose of the culprit.

Bibliography

Amery, Heather and Patricia Vanags. *The Usborne Time Traveller Book of Rome & Romans*. Usborne, 1993.

Ancient Rome. See Through History Series. Hanlyn Children's Books, 1992.

Chilholm, Jane. *Living in Roman Times*. Usborne First History. Usborne: 1987.

Connolly, Peter. *Pompeii*. Oxford Press, 1990.

Cohen, Daniel. *Ancient Rome*. Doubleday Book for Young Readers. Delacorte Press; Bantam Doubleday Dll, New York: 1992.

Etienne, Robert. *Pompeii, The Day a City Died*. Harry N. Abrams, Inc., New York, 1992.

Ganeri, Anita. *How Would You Survive as an Ancient Roman?* Franklin Watts/Grolier Publishing, 1995.

Grant, M. *History of Rome*. New York: Scribner, 1980.

James, Simon. *Ancient Rome*. See Through History. Viking Press, 1992.

James, Simon. *Ancient Rome*. Eyewitness Books. Alfred A. Knopf, New York, 1990.

Marks, Antony. *The Romans*. The Usborne Illustrated World History. Usborne, 1990.

Olgivie, R.M. *Roman Literature and Society*. New York: Penguin, 1980.

Peris Carme. *The Greek and Roman Eras*. Journey Through History. Barron's, 1988.

The Romans. History as Evidence Series. Kingfisher, 1992.

Rome and the Ancient World. Illustrated History of the World Series. Simon & Schuster, 1991.

Rome in the Time of Augustus. Making History Series. Simon & Schuster, 1993.

Sekunda, Nick. *Republican Roman Army*. Men-at-Arms Series. Osprey, London, 1996.

Webster, G. *Roman Imperial Army*. New York: Barnes & Noble, Third Edition, 1985.

Wolff, H. *Roman Law*. U. of Okla., Norman, Okla.: 1985.

Computer Software

Ancient Civilizations: Greece and Rome. CD-ROM. National Geographic Society.

Internet Resources

The Forvm Romanvm http://library.advanced.org/11402